OF
CASTLEKNOCK

JIM O'HANLON

NEW ISLAND

THE BUDDHIST OF CASTLEKNOCK
First published 2007
by New Island
2 Brookside
Dundrum Road
Dublin 14
www.newisland.ie

Copyright © 2007 Jim O'Hanlon

The author has asserted his moral rights.

ISBN 978-1-904301-99-8

All rights reserved. The material in this publication is protected by copyright law. Except as may be permitted by law, no part of the material may be reproduced (including by storage in a retrieval system) or transmitted in any form or by any means; adapted; rented or lent without the written permission of the copyright owners.

'For What Died the Sons of Róisín' by Luke Kelly is reproduced by kind permission of Mary Kelly.

Caution: applications for performance, etc., by amateurs or professionals, should be made before rehearsals begin, to the author's agent, Ken McReddie Ltd, 36–40 Glasshouse Street, London, W1B 5DL. No performance may be given unless a licence has been obtained.

British Library Cataloguing in Publication Data. A CIP catalogue record for this book is available from the British Library.

Printed in the UK by Athenaeum Press Ltd., Gateshead, Tyne & Wear

New Island received financial assistance from
The Arts Council (An Chomhairle Ealaíon), Dublin, Ireland.

10 9 8 7 6 5 4 3 2 1

SUFFOLK COUNTY LIBRARIES & HERITAGE	
07039395	
HJ	13/07/2007
F	£7.99

Characters
(in order of appearance)

DJ – *real name Julian, aged fifteen*
Edie Sullivan – *early fifties*
Sean – *Edie's husband*
Tara – *Edie and Sean's daughter, thirty*
Edward – *their son, late twenties*
John – *Edward's younger brother, mid-twenties*
Rai – *John's girlfriend, twenty-six*
Uncle Jimmy – *late fifties*
Auntie Kathleen – *Edie's older sister, married to* **Uncle Jimmy**

Act One takes place on Christmas Eve
Act Two takes place on Christmas Day
Act Three, Scene i takes place on St Stephen's Day
Act Three, Scene ii takes place a week or so later

Act One

A suburban sitting room in Dublin. This is the 'Good Room', and reflects the comfortably-off surroundings of a well-to-do, middle-class, professional home. Copious – but tastefully arranged – Christmas decorations hang along the upper reaches of the three visible walls of the room. In the back wall, to the right of centre, a door leads out into the hallway, some of which is visible to the audience. In the stage right wall is a large fireplace with mantlepiece. On the mantlepiece, various photographs of the family at salient points in their shared lives – graduations, a wedding photograph, photos of babies. At right angles to the fireplace is a plush sofa, and downstage right of the fireplace is an armchair. There is another armchair centre stage, facing the fireplace. To the left of the door into the hall is a large, beautifully decorated Christmas tree. Elsewhere, boxes of Christmas lights and other decorations are strewn around the room. **DJ** *(short for DJ Jules – real name Julian) enters stage left in his boxer shorts.* **DJ** *is fifteen, and sports a trendy fifteen-year-old's haircut. He searches frantically but cursorily among the boxes of decorations then gives up and goes to the door at the back of the stage and calls upstairs.*

DJ Mum!

Edie (*off*) What?

DJ Have you seen my Tommy's?

Edie (*off*) Your what?

DJ My jeans. My Tommy Hilfigers!

Edie (*off*) I put them in the wash.

DJ Mum! What did you do that for?

Edie (*off*) Because they were filthy.

DJ (*under his breath*) For fuck's sake!

At that moment **Edie** *appears in from the hallway.* **Edie** *is in her early fifties, a precise, well-spoken woman dressed in an expensive, if slightly conservative, matching top and skirt.*

Edie What did you say?

DJ Nothing.

Edie Yes, you did.

DJ No, I didn't. I just said where's my Tommy Hilfigers.

Edie I will not tolerate that language in this house, Julian. Have you put the wreath up on the front door yet?

DJ No.

Edie Julian! John and Edward will be here any minute and we still don't have a wreath on the door to greet them.

DJ So?

Edie So, they're coming home for Christmas, and I want the place looking nice for them.

The Buddhist of Castleknock

DJ What do they care about a bloody wreath for? They're not twelve, you know.

Edie Just stop complaining and get it out of the basket there.

DJ I hate putting the wreath up. It never stays – it always falls down.

Edie Julian, I'm asking you to do one little job for me. Over the whole of the Christmas. You haven't lifted a finger since you got your holidays.

DJ Right, that's it! If you're going to go round telling total lies and libelling me, I'm out of here!

Edie Julian! Julian, come back here! JULIAN!

But he's gone.

Edie (*under her breath*) For fuck's sake!

Sean *appears and smiles sweetly, but says nothing.* **Sean** *is a couple of years older than* **Edie**, *with a relaxed, easy demeanour.*

Edie I'm telling you, I'm at the end of my tether with him. If he ruins this Christmas with his carry on that's it – he's going to boarding school.

Sean *goes to pick up the paper.*

Edie You're not thinking of sitting down? I asked you to put the wreath on the door an hour ago.

Sean I thought you asked Julian to do it.

Edie Well, now I'm asking you.

Sean Where is it?

Edie In the basket there. And be careful with it. You know how delicate it is.

Sean If it's so delicate, maybe we shouldn't bother putting it up.

Edie Look, are you going to hang the confounded wreath or do I have to do that myself too?

Sean *crosses to the decorations box and takes out a home-made wreath which* **Edie** *has made. He goes to the front door, opens it and starts to hang the wreath on the door knocker.* **Edie**, *meanwhile, crosses to the record player and takes an LP of Christmas songs out of its sleeve. She places the record on the turntable. A crackly recording of 'I'm Dreaming of a White Christmas' begins to play.* **Edie** *stands listening to it for a couple of moments. Then she pulls over a chair and begins hanging the last bits of holly on the walls.*

Edie Thank God for Tara, that's all I can say. I don't know what I would have done without her this Christmas. I don't think she's sat down since she got here. Poor love – she's been that busy helping me she hasn't even had a chance to wrap her presents. No more than I have myself. Quick, Sean – hand me over some of those tags there on the mantlepiece.

Sean Lord God, such commotion and combobulation! You'd swear we were expecting the Pope himself to drop by.

Edie They hate coming home and finding nothing ready, Sean.

Sean Pity about them.

Edie That reminds me – did you manage to fix that leaky tap in the bathroom?

Sean I did a patch-up job. We'll need to get a plumber in to have a look at it after Christmas.

Edie (*looks at her watch*) Do you think it's too late to get a plumber now?

Sean Edie, it's Christmas Eve! Anyway, I told you – I've done a temporary job. You just have to be careful to give it a good hard twist at the end.

Edie I'm sorry, love. I know I'm flapping. I'm just excited is all. I just want everything to be … perfect. (*A beat*) Especially if …

Sean If what?

Edie Especially if it's going to be our last Christmas together. As a family. I'm not saying it is … for definite. But it could be. They're all away now, and they'll start coming back less and less, and … (*She trails off sadly*)

Sean You've done everything you possibly could, love. You've got a fantastic Christmas tree, with … with beautiful decorations and lights and whatnot. (*A beat*) It's down to them now.

A beat

Edie You don't think the tree is lopsided?

Sean (*not even looking at the tree*) Edie, it's fine. Honestly – you're such a worrier. Everything will be grand.

Edie I hope so. I couldn't bear it if this did turn out to be our last Christmas together and it was a disaster. Especially with John's new girlfriend coming.

Sean What's her name again?

Edie Rai.

Sean Rai – Christ, sounds like a fella.

Edie Oh don't, Sean. Can you imagine it?

Sean You'd never know with John.

Edie Get away out of that, you, and stop your messing.

Sean *laughs.*

Sean Anyway, fellow, female or a bit of both – you'd think he'd have given us a bit more notice.

Edie He told me last week … I just … forgot to mention it in all the commotion.

Sean (*shrugs*) It doesn't bother me. (*A beat*) Does it bother you?

Edie No. (*A beat*) Although I was a bit taken aback when he asked if he could bring her. I always think of Christmas as a family time.

Sean Maybe that's what he's bringing her over to tell us.

Edie What?

Sean That she's about to become a part of our family.

Edie We haven't even met her yet!

Sean Or that we can expect another member of the family in nine months' time.

Edie God, Sean, don't say that – even for a joke. My nerves would never stand it.

Sean Brace yourself to inherit two brand new family members, Edie Sullivan – three if it's twins!

Edie Ach, don't be ridiculous, Sean – sure, they only know each other a couple of months. Anyway, the only reason she's coming here is that her family have gone away to Kenya for the Christmas.

Sean Kenya? They must be gone on a safari or something. Jays, they can't be short of a few bob to be going on safari in Kenya. I don't see the attraction myself. What would anyone want to spend Christmas in Kenya for?

Edie I've no idea. They must like the sun, I suppose. Some people do, apparently.

Sean I could never go away for Christmas. I'd miss my turkey and ham sandwiches and my bottle of Guinness with Jimmy and Kathleen on St Stephen's Day.

Edie That'd be you all right. A real homebird.

Sean Sure, why wouldn't I be? Don't I live in the loveliest of homes in the loveliest of countries, as the fella said?

Edie And which fellow would that be when he's at home?

Sean Some French fella – but he must have been living in Ireland at the time.

Edie Mm.

A pause, as **Edie** *gets on with putting up the last of the decorations*

Sean Would you say in Kenya Santy still wears that big red suit? It must get awful warm.

Edie Here, pass me over that holly there and don't mind Santy and his big red suit.

As **Sean** *crosses to get the holly,* **Tara** *appears down the stairs.* **Tara** *is* **Edie** *and* **Sean's** *eldest child. She is about thirty years old. She looks drawn today – her eyes are red from crying, and she looks tired.*

Edie (*gentle*) Did you get through to Paudge?

Tara (*wiping away a tear*) Yes.

Edie   And?

Tara   Sean Óg's fine. Says to say Happy Christmas.

Edie   Ah. Did you hear that, Sean? Sean Óg says to say Happy Christmas to his Granny and Grandad.

Sean   Good man himself.

Tara   He says he'd much rather be here for Christmas.

Sean   I'm sure he would – stuck up there in the back end of Antrim with that jackass of a husband of yours.

Tara   I was so looking forward to this Christmas – with the boys back, and John's new girlfriend, and now …

Edie   Ssh, Tara, love. We'll still have a wonderful time. I promise you.

She breaks off as there's a ring on the doorbell.

Edie   Jesus, Mary and Joseph, that'll be them now. And I haven't a thing ready!

Sean   What do you mean, you haven't a thing ready? The bloody place looks like Santa's feckin' grotto!

Edie   Sean! There's no need to swear. (*Indicating* **Tara**) Not in front of the children.

Tara   Mum, I'm thirty years of age!

Edie That's no reason to stop giving you moral guidance, Tara love. (*A beat*) I'm sorry, I didn't mean that.

A beat.

Edie Sean, run out there and put the kettle on like a good man and I'll get the door.

And she starts to make for the front door.

Tara I'll get it.

Edie Are you sure?

Tara Mum, I'm fine. Honestly. (**Edie** *nods. A beat*) And Mum? (**Edie** *turns*) Thanks. I mean it. You've been great since … well, since the whole thing.

Edie You can stay as long as you like, pet. Can't she, Sean?

Sean Of course you can, love.

Tara Thanks.

Another ring on the doorbell.

Tara Coming!

Edie *crosses to the record player and switches it off as* **Tara** *answers the door to* **Edward**. **Edward** *is in his late twenties, tall, broad-shouldered and confident. The family trickster,* **Edward** *is sporting a red Santa hat and white beard which almost completely obscures his face.*

The Buddhist of Castleknock

Edward Ho Ho Ho! Ho Ho Ho! Are there any good children in this house or is this a job for Santy's sack of coal?

Edward *throws a big bag full of presents into the house ahead of him.*

Edie Ach, would you look at him! Edward!

Edward *takes off his beard.*

Edward You recognised me! What was it – the broad shoulders and the lean torso? How're you, Mammy?

And he gives **Edie** *a kiss.*

Edie Happy Christmas, love.

Edward How're ye, Da? Hey, nice tree.

Edie (*beaming, delighted*) Do you like it? I picked it out myself.

Edward It's great. Little bit lopsided, but apart from that it looks great.

Edie It's not lopsided.

Edward Well, not lopsided exactly … but it definitely leans to the right.

Edie *inclines her head and looks at the tree in an effort to gauge whether or not it is in fact leaning.* **Edward**, *meanwhile, takes off his coat.*

Edward No sign of John and – what's-her-name?

Edie Rai.

Sean If indeed it is a her.

Tara Dad reckons Rai's a fella.

Sean Well, you can count on the thumbs of one hand the number of girlfriends John has brought home …

Edie Ah Sean, stop your messing. Your Dad's such a messer.

Tara So what if Rai is a fella? It's the new Ireland, now don't forget, Dad – liberal, secular and infinitely tolerant.

Sean New Ireland my arse!

Edie Sean!

Sean Well, it seems anything goes, nowadays.

Tara Go away out of that, Daddy. I know you – you're as liberal as the next fella. He just likes to play the part of the gruff Irish Father, don't you, Daddy? Still and all, can you imagine (*adopts a pose, and a camp, lispy voice*) Daddy, this is my extra special friend Rai – Rai, my pater Sean!

They laugh raucously, all except **Edward**, *who smiles politely.*

Edward (*dry*) Ah yes. Welcome to the new Ireland.

The doorbell rings again.

Edie That'll be them now. So quit your messing you two, and don't be disgracing me in front of the poor girl.

Sean and **Tara** *cease their joking as* **Edie** *opens the front door to* **John**. **John** *is* **Edward***'s younger brother – slightly smaller and thinner than his elder brother, he is none the less handsome, despite his somewhat scruffy appearance.*

Edie John!

John Hiya, Mum.

John *moves out of the way to allow* **Rai** *to enter.* **Rai** *is about twenty-six, English, of African extraction.*

John Hiya, Dad. Mum, this is Rai. Rai – this is my Mum, Edie, and my Dad, Sean.

Rai Hiya.

A brief pause, as **Edie** *and* **Sean** *adjust their stride. Any hesitation – if indeed there even is a moment's hesitation – is quickly covered over by the effusiveness of their welcomes.*

Sean How are you, Rai? You're very welcome.

Edie You must be exhausted.

Rai I'm pretty knackered all right. We were delayed nearly three and a half hours at the airport. With the snow, you know?

Edie You poor things. Still, wouldn't it be wonderful if we got a white Christmas here? We haven't had a white Christmas in I don't know how long.

Edward According to the weather forecast it's going the other way. They've forecast rain here for tomorrow.

Edie Have you met John's brother, Rai – our resident Harbinger of Doom?

Rai Hiya. Edward?

Edward That's right. The good-looking one.

Rai John's told me a lot about you.

Edward All good, I hope.

Rai Well, fair to middling, as you might say here in Ireland.

Edward *laughs.*

Edward You're picking up the lingo, anyway.

Rai Is it any wonder, living with John?

Edie We'll have you turned into a nice Irish colleen soon enough, Rai, don't you worry.

John (*quickly*) And this is Tara. Tara – Rai.

Rai Pleased to meet you, Tara.

Tara Likewise.

Edie Will you have a cup of tea? You must be parched after all the travelling.

Rai Well, if you're making one …

Edie Tara, run out there and put the kettle on for John and Rai, like a good girl. (*To* **Rai**) I did ask Sean to do it, but I may as well be talking to the back end of a donkey for all the good it does me.

Rai If it's any trouble …

Edie It's no trouble at all, is it Tara?

Tara No. No trouble.

Rai Do you want a hand? Because I could—

Edie You sit down there and make yourself comfortable, Rai. You've had a long journey.

Rai (*to* **Tara**) Well, if you're sure … ?

Tara I won't be a minute.

Tara *exits right towards the kitchen to make the tea. A brief silence.*

Rai It's great to put a face to the names, you know? John talks about you all the time. It's nice to actually meet you all properly.

Sean Well – are we uglier or better looking than you expected?

Rai (*laughs*) Much better looking.

Sean Been talking us down again, have you, John?

John Would I?

They laugh. A moment's silence. **Rai** *smiles across at* **John**, *who smiles awkardly back.*

Edie Well, all I can say is it's great to have you all here for the Christmas. Isn't it, Sean?

Sean It is, love.

Edie You get a bit older, these are the things that keep you going. Having your family around at times like Christmas.

Rai I hope I'm not intruding. John said—

Edie Not at all, Rai. We're delighted to have you. Aren't we, Sean?

Sean We are of course, love. Thrilled.

Rai That's very kind of you.

Tara What do you think of the tree, Johnny? Edward reckons it leans.

John *inclines his head and looks at it.*

John I suppose it does a bit. But sure, that can easily be rectified.

Tara Apparently not. Apparently it's doomed to lean.

The Buddhist of Castleknock

Edward The leaning Christmas tree of Castleknock, wha'?

John Still, it'd be worth shifting the base around anyway to see if there's a bushier side. It's a bit bare towards the bottom.

Tara And the top. Sure, there are hardly any branches up the top.

Edie God, yous are all very pass-remarkable. I spent hours in a wet, muddy garden centre choosing that tree. I bet you don't stand around criticising the Christmas tree your mother chose, do you Rai?

Rai Er ... no. No.

Edie Of course you don't. You probably wouldn't dare. But this lot ...

Edward It's a lovely tree, Mum. And you have the place looking fabulous. Hasn't she?

John 'Course she does. It looks great. Although I meant to say – the wreath on the door has fallen off.

Edie Ah Sean, did you not put it up properly? (*to* **Rai**) The one job I leave to somebody else ...

Sean I was only doing it because Julian was nowhere to be seen!

John That'd be Julian, all right.

Edward (*to* **Rai**) You haven't met DJ Jules yet?

Rai DJ Jules?

John Wait till you see him. You'd swear he'd never left the ghettoes of Los Angeles.

Edward Except for the fact of his being white as the driven snow.

Edie Edward!

Edward What?

Edie *nods discretely in* **Rai**'s *direction.*

Edward What's Rai got to do with DJ being white?

Sean (*quickly*) Well if he doesn't get here soon, the great white hope of Irish rap music is going to miss coming to midnight mass.

Edward (*good-humoured*) I'm sure that's the idea.

Edie He always does this. Disappears straight after his dinner and you don't see sight nor sound of him until God knows when. And we still haven't put Mammy's Angel on the top of the tree.

Sean You put another decoration on that tree and it'll collapse!

Edie (*to* **Rai**, *ignoring* **Sean**) It's a family tradition. On Christmas Eve, when everyone's back, the youngest member of the family puts Mammy's Angel on the top of the tree. As a sort of a way of putting the finishing touches to the decorations, and to remind us of the true meaning of Christmas.

Rai That's ... lovely.

Edie The whole thing's gone so commercialised these days, I think it's nice to remind ourselves what we're really celebrating.

Rai Absolutely.

Edie We call it Mammy's Angel because it used to belong to my mother and she left it to the kids when she died.

Edward Some people get thousands of pounds when their grandmother dies, or a house, or a car. We got a glass angel from Hector Grey's.

Edie Don't mind him, Rai. It's not glass. It's Waterford Crystal. (*To* **Edward**) Get it out of the drawer there, Edward, till we show it to Rai. It's in the bottom drawer, the one with all the photo albums.

Edward *crosses to get the angel out of the drawer.*

Edie You'll love it, Rai – it's just beautiful. Isn't it, Tara?

Tara It is, Mum. (*To* **Rai**, *regarding the tea*) Milk?

Rai Please.

Edward *comes back with the angel, which is wrapped in a piece of white linen.*

Edward Jays, Mum, it looks like you've got it in a funeral shroud. Is it dead?

Edie (*unwrapping the angel*) He certainly is not. He's alive and well and living in Castleknock.

Edward How do you know if an angel's a 'he' or a 'she'?

Tara Same way as you do for normal people, I suppose.

Edward (*in mock horror*) Ah no, they don't … ? Surely not …? (*Examining the angel*) Where is it …?

Edie (*to* **Rai**, *ignoring* **Edward** *as she holds the angel up for* **Rai**'*s approval*) What do you think?

Rai It's … beautiful.

Edie It's an antique. It's nearly a hundred years old.

John And worth an awful lot of money, apparently.

Rai Yeah?

John They had it valued last year. The whole thing is worth over €400.

DJ That yoke?! No way!

The others turn to see **DJ** *who has entered stage left and is tip-toeing in the direction of the hall, hoping to escape unnoticed.*

Edie Where have you been?

The Buddhist of Castleknock

DJ Out. (*To* **John**) Is it really worth over over €400?

John That's what the antique dealer said.

DJ Bloody hell!

Edie Julian!

DJ Sorry. But €400 – that's unbelievable.

Sean Well, there you have it. That's what the fella said.

Edie Julian, did you say hello to Rai?

DJ (*grunts*) How're'ye.

Edie Anyway, we'd never sell it. Ever. It gets passed on to the eldest daughter – it's come right down through the maternal line from my great-grandmother.

Rai Like African custom.

Edie Like … ?

Rai In many African countries, it's the maternal line which is important – kids take their mother's names and that. Have done for centuries.

Edie Quite right, too. I'm afraid we haven't quite developed that far in Ireland yet. (*She turns and spots* **DJ** *about to head out the front door again*) Where do you think you're going?

DJ Tommy's.

Edie Oh no you're not. We're all going to do the Angel ceremony, and then we're off to midnight mass.

DJ Mum!

Edie I'm not arguing, Julian. You know the rules. Christmas Eve is family time. Isn't that right, Rai?

Rai Well …

Edie You see? Even Rai agrees with me. Right – everyone – gather round. Julian. As the youngest member of the family—

Edward As far as we know …

Edie Edward, please! (*To* **DJ**) As the youngest member of the family, you get to put Mammy's Angel on the top of the Christmas tree.

DJ (*sarcastic*) Whoopee!

Sean Julian!

Edie Sean – pass me over the Baby Jesus there, please. He's on the mantlepiece beside the matches.

Sean *crosses to the mantlepiece to get the statue of the Baby Jesus. He hands it to* **DJ***, who sighs and reluctantly stands on the chair* **Edward** *has dragged into position for him by the tree. Suddenly,* **DJ** *lets out a cry and crumples his legs suddenly as if he's dropped the Angel.*

Edie Julian!

DJ Fooled yous!

Edie It's not funny, Julian. That Angel is nearly a hundred years old. Now place him gently on the top of the tree, and no more fooling around.

DJ *leans up and starts to put the angel at the apex of the Christmas tree.*

Edie Sean?

Sean Hm? Oh, yes. Sorry.

Sean *closes his eyes and prepares to pray.*

Edie Gently, Julian! I didn't say fire him on! That's Mammy's Angel you have there!

DJ Sorry!

Edward (*sings*) He's got the whole world …

John *and* **Edward** In his hands!

Edie Edward! Sorry, Sean. On you go.

Sean Lord, we place this statue of Mammy's Angel on the top of our Christmas tree—

Edward Our rather beautiful, non-leaning Christmas tree—

Sean We place this statue on the top of the tree as a reminder of the true meaning of Christmas. In doing so, we ask you to watch over us as Mammy's Angel watches over our living room, and keep us safe over the Christmas period, so that in the midst of all the fun and the merriement—

Edward   And the booze—

Edie   Edward!

Sean   That in the midst of all the celebrations we may not lose sight of the true essence of Christmas – the birth of Jesus Christ our Lord. Amen.

Others   Amen.

Edie *opens her eyes.*

Edie   Right then. All hold hands.

They do so, with various levels of discomfort and embarrassment.

DJ   This is so embarrassing! Nobody else I know has to do stuff like this at Christmas!

Edie   They don't know what they're missing out on, then. Isn't that right, Rai?

Rai *smiles politely.*

Sean   Besides, it's tradition.

DJ   So?

Sean   So we do it every year.

DJ Why?

Sean We just do, that's all.

Edie Whose turn is it to choose this year?

John I chose last year.

Edward And I chose the year before that.

Tara No, you didn't. I chose two years ago.

Edward You did not. I remember I chose 'I Saw Mommy Kissing Santa Claus' and it was vetoed because Dad said it wasn't a carol.

Edie Come on, Tara, love, it doesn't matter. You choose.

Tara All right. But I'm telling you, I chose two years ago. So it couldn't possibly be my turn to—

Sean Ara, Tara, pick a feckin' carol, will you, and let's start singing!

Edie Sean, please. (*She nods towards the crib on the dresser*) Not in front of the Baby Jesus.

Sean Look, I'll bloody pick one!

Edie No, it has to be one of the children. That's the tradition.

John DJ, you pick.

Edward And none of your rap numbers.

DJ I don't know any carols.

Edie Of course you do. What about 'Away in a Manger'?

DJ Oh, yeah.

Edie So is that it?

DJ What?

Edie Is that your pick?

DJ Yeah. I suppose.

Sean Right then. At last. 'Away in a Manger', picked by Julian.

DJ *throws his eyes to heaven.*

Edie On the count of three. One, two—

Tara Hang on, what about Rai?

Edie What about her?

Tara (*to* **Rai**) Do you know 'Away in a Manger'?

Rai Don't worry about me.

Edie Are you sure, Rai, love? Because we can always pick another one.

Sean Jesus preserve us – we'll be here till New Year if we've to pick another one!

Rai Honestly, don't worry about me. I don't … I don't really know any Christmas carols, to be honest with you.

Edie Oh. I see.

A pause.

Sean Look, are we going to sing or aren't we?

Tara Right. On the count of three. One, two—

Edward Hold on.

Sean (*losing patience*) What now, Edward?

Edward Shouldn't we pick a key?

Sean What?

Edward Should we not decide on a key we can all sing in?

Edie Edward, we've never had this problem before.

Edward Before was different.

Edie How was it?

Edward Before, DJ's balls hadn't dropped.

DJ Right, I'm out of here!

DJ *lets go of whoever's hand he's holding and heads for the front door.*

Edie Edward!

Edward Ah here, DJ, I was only joking you.

DJ No, I'm not staying around here to be insulted!

Edie He was only joking, Julian. Weren't you, Edward?

Edward 'Course I was. Come on and join in the festivities, DJ.

DJ No! It's bad enough having to stand around holding hands like a whole family of poofs without being insulted as well!

Edward I was only having a laugh. It's Christmas – where's your sense of humour?

Edie He's probably embarrassed to sing now his voice has broken – is that it? Is that why you're a bit touchy?

DJ I'm not touchy! I'm just f—

Sean (*quickly*) Come on, for Jaysus sake, and let's sing the feckin' song! Are you right? Julian?

DJ *reluctantly comes back and rejoins the group.*

DJ One more word out of him and I'm going, I'm telling you!

Edward I promise – I won't say another word.

Sean Right. Anyone else with anything to say before we start? No? Good. On the count of three, in the key of Dad.

DJ Tell him he's not funny.

Sean One, two, three.

They start to sing, uncertainly at first, but with increasing gusto – all except **DJ** *and* **Rai**, *who doesn't know the words.*

All   Away in a manger
               No crib for a bed … *etc.*

The others keep singing as **Edie** *breaks off.*

Edie Julian!

DJ What?

Edie Sing!

DJ I am singing.

Edie Well, sing louder. I can't hear you. (*sings*) … lay down his sweet head.

DJ (*under his breath before he starts singing*) Fuck's sake.

Edie *shoots* **DJ** *a look but continues singing.*

All   The stars in the bright sky
               Look down where he lay

> The little Lord Jesus
> Asleep in the hay

When they reach the end of the first verse, they all stop singing apart from **Edie**, *who continues tunefully, spiritually with the second verse, eyes closed.* **Sean** *joins in as best he can – but he can only remember the odd phrase here and there.*

Edie (*sings*) The cattle are lowing
> The baby awake
> The little Lord Jesus
> No crying he makes
> I love you, Lord Jesus
> And ask you to stay
> Close by me forever
> And love me I pray

Edie *and* **Sean** *finish the second verse together.*

Edward Well done, Mum. That was lovely.

Rai You've got a beautiful voice, Mrs Sullivan.

Edie (*delighted*) Thank you, love. Although you should hear Sean singing properly. Now there's a voice. When he knows all the words.

Sean It's just that second verse. I'm never sure of the second verse.

Edie You don't say.

John But he's a great voice when he puts his mind to it, don't you, Da?

Sean Ach, well – it wasn't a bad voice once. Though it isn't a patch on your Uncle Jimmy's. Now there's a voice for singing the ballads.

Edie You'll hear Uncle Jimmy singing on St Stephen's Day. They always come over for a bit of Christmas cake and a sing-song on St Stephen's Day.

John (*to* **Rai**) Boxing Day.

Edie Of course, you don't call it St Stephen's Day, do you? Boxing Day. What an odd name for a day. I wonder where that came from?

Rai Search me. I never knew it was called anything else.

At some point during this next conversation, **DJ** *sneaks up to his bedroom.*

Edie Clearing up the boxes all the Christmas presents came in, maybe. Or putting them back into their boxes.

Edward Internecine boxing matches because twenty-four hours cooped up together has finally driven everyone around the bend?

Tara Why do you always have to be so negative, Edward? We're having a perfectly nice time here.

Edward I do apologise.

Edie (*quickly*) I suppose there must be some reason it's called Boxing Day. Otherwise they'd have just stuck with St Stephen's Day, wouldn't they?

Edward Which came first, eh – the chicken or the egg?

Sean (*quickly*) Listen, we're going to miss midnight mass if we don't get a move on. It's nearly ten past ten.

Edward (*explaining to* **Rai**) Midnight mass starts at half ten around here. A local peculiarity.

Edie It's so the children can come too. They get too tired if it starts later than half ten.

Rai Ah.

Edie You'll just have time to put your stuff up in your rooms, and then we'll have to be off. John, show Rai where she's going to be sleeping.

John Where *is* she going to be sleeping?

Edie I've put her up in Tara's old room. It's the nicest room.

Rai What about … ?

Edie Tara's sleeping in the spare room. She doesn't mind at all, do you, love?

Tara No.

Edie Edward, I've put you in with Julian, and John, you can sleep on the camp bed down here.

Rai I can sleep on the camp bed. I don't mind.

Edie (*almost aggressive*) You most certainly cannot! This is your first visit to Ireland – how could I send you back to your mother telling her you were made to sleep on a camp bed in the living room?

Rai Thank you. Thank you all. You've all been most welcoming.

Sean We need to get a move on or we'll be dead late.

John I'll show you your room.

They head off up the stairs, **John** *helping* **Rai** *to carry her bags.* **Edward** *follows them, also carrying his bags.* **Tara** *exits stage left towards the kitchen to get her coat. A beat. It is as if* **Edie** *is waiting until the others have disappeared upstairs before speaking. When she does speak, she does so very tentatively.*

Edie So. What do you think?

Sean Of what?

Edie Of Rai. Do you like her?

Sean Of course.

Edie There's no 'of course' about it. You don't have to like her.

Sean She's John's girlfriend. So of course I like her. (*A beat*) Why – don't you like her?

Edie I do. She seems like a lovely girl.

Sean There you are then.

A beat.

Sean Still, she's certainly ... how can I put it ... she's certainly more ... well ... *tanned* than I expected.

Edie Sean!

Sean I'm not saying there's anything wrong with that. On the contrary, I think it's quite ... exciting. But there's no point in pretending we haven't noticed.

Edie It doesn't bother you?

Sean Not in the least. You?

Edie Good Lord, no.

Sean Great. I thought you might be ...

Edie Well, I'm not.

Sean Great. That's ... great.

A pause. **Sean** *exits to the hall to get his and* **Edie***'s coats. When he comes back, he's laughing gently to himself.*

Edie What?

Sean I'm just thinking – could you imagine Jimmy and Kathleen if their Carmel brought home ... you know ... a coloured boyfriend?

Edie I wouldn't have thought they'd bat an eyelid.

Sean Kathleen would. Kathleen's suspicious of anyone who wasn't born in Castleknock village!

Edie (*defensive*) It's different for a girl.

Sean Get away out of that. You're just saying that because Kathleen's your sister.

Edie You think Jimmy would be any better?

Sean I think he'd be worse! I love him dearly, but he's a terrible old bigot, is Jimmy.

Edie I hope it's OK on Stephen's Day.

Sean It'll be fine. They'll be too polite to say anything. Trust me.

A beat. **Sean** *and* **Edie** *look as if they might kiss, but at that moment, the others appear down the stairs.*

Edie (*flapping a little, embarrassed*) Are we right, so? (*Looking around her*) Where's Julian? Julian! (*But* **DJ**'*s gone flying out the front door ahead of her*) I don't believe it – he's disappeared again! The minute I take my eyes off him he's gone, the little ... !

Sean We'll just have to go without him. There won't be a seat left if we don't get the skids under us.

Tara And believe me, Rai, you do not want to have to stand through one of Father Aidan's Christmas sermons.

Rai (*awkward*) I hope you don't think I'm being rude, but – I think I might give midnight mass a miss.

Edie Oh?

Rai If that's all right. I'm … I'm just exhausted with all the travelling.

Edie Oh. What a pity. Father Aidan does a lovely midnight mass. And the carol singing is beautiful, isn't it, John?

Rai I'm sure it's lovely, Mrs Sullivan, I just …

John Rai isn't Catholic, Mum.

Edie Oh. (*A beat*) Well, that doesn't mean she couldn't come to midnight mass. Father Aidan is a great supporter of ecumenism.

Rai Honestly, I'm really knackered, Mrs Sullivan …

Edie I hate leaving you here alone on your first night with us. It seems so … inhospitable.

Rai I'll be fine. I think I'll just go straight to bed.

Edie Well, if you're sure. There's tea bags in the kitchen, in the press over the dishwasher. Just make yourself completely at home.

Rai Thank you. I will.

A pause.

Edie Right then. Everyone else ready?

Edward (*yawning*)   You know, I'm pretty bushed myself …

Edie (*ushering him towards the door*)   Out!

Edward *sighs, reluctantly accepting his fate.*

Edward   If we're not back in a couple of hours, Rai, send in the troops.

Rai   Have fun.

Sean   Right then. Eyes front. Forwaaard march!

They all start to file out. **John** *lingers behind.*

John   Mum …

Edie   What is it now, John? We're going to miss mass altogether if we don't get a move on.

John   The thing is, I don't think I'm going to come either.

Edie   Why on earth not? We always go to midnight mass on Christmas eve.

John   The thing is, Mum … I don't think I'm really going to be celebrating Christmas this year. I mean, not in the way that—

Edie   Not celebrate? What are you talking about, John?

Sean *reappears at the door to the living room.*

Sean Are yous right?

John I'm not a Catholic any more, Mum. So I don't … believe in Christmas. (*A beat, as* **Edie** *looks at him uncomprehendingly*) I've become a Buddhist.

Edie Jesus, Mary and Joseph.

Blackout.

Act Two

Scene One

It is Christmas Day, in the early afternoon. As the lights come up, **John** *and* **Rai** *enter.* **John** *is carrying two bottles of champagne.* **Rai** *carries a bag full of presents.*

John Well, so much for a white Christmas. Lashing rain and a gale-force wind.

Rai Your mother will be disappointed.

John But not surprised. I don't think there's been a white Christmas in Ireland in living memory.

Rai Doesn't stop people hoping, though, does it? Shall I put the presents under the tree?

John Yeah, just pile them in the back there with the others. I'll put these in the fridge.

Rai *crosses to the Christmas tree and puts her presents under it, along with all the others. When she's finished, she stands looking up at the Angel on the top of the tree. After a couple of seconds,* **John** *reappears from the kitchen, still clutching his bottles of champagne.*

John Fridge is chock-a-block. There isn't room to fit a thimbleful of champagne, let alone two bottles.

He pulls up as he notices **Rai** *looking up at the Angel on top of the tree.*

John Nice, isn't it.

Rai It's beautiful.

John Despite the connotations?

Rai You know, it's a funny thing. I can't stand nearly everything the Catholic Church represents – no offence, like – but somehow, Catholic iconography always … moves me in some way.

John I know what you mean.

They stand looking up at the Angel for a couple of seconds.

Rai Does it make you regret converting to Buddhism? Missing out on the whole Christmas thing?

John It's only the religious side. We can still join in the rest of the celebrations.

Rai I thought that was the whole point of Christmas – the religious side?

John How many people do you know who celebrate Christmas as Jesus' birthday?

Rai Your Mum does. And your Dad.

John Good, so we're up to two. Two out of a world population of several billion. What's that in percentage terms?

Rai Edward and Tara.

John Tara, maybe. Though I suspect with her it's as much for an easy life as out of any real conviction.

Rai And Edward?

John I don't know about Edward – I can't work him out. (*A beat*) So that gives us two definites, a possible and a maybe. And the rest of the world just gets drunk and stuffs its face with turkey.

Rai *laughs. A beat.*

Rai I think she took it quite well. From the way you were talking, I thought we might have been packing our bags by now. Your dad looked a bit taken aback.

John All he'd be worried about is having his rhythm upset. Especially at Christmas. Speaking of which …

Rai What?

John I thought we could maybe nip up to your room for twenty minutes.

Rai (*suggestive*) Oh yeah?

John Get a spot of meditation in before dinner. The calm before the storm.

Rai Bloody hell. The zeal of the convert …

John I'll stick an oul' Christmas record on, drown out the sounds. I think Buddhist chanting on Christmas Day might just be that one little step too far.

John *starts searching among the record collection for an album of Christmas songs.* **Rai** *comes up behind him sexily.*

Rai We don't have to chant, John. We could always—

John Here we are. Perfect. *Sing-alonga-Christmas – All your Favourite Christmas Hits.*

He takes the record from its sleeve, puts it on the turntable, and carefully places the needle down on it. The record crackles, then an old, very scratched recording of 'Rudolph the Red-Nosed Reindeer' starts up.

John There we go. They won't hear a thing now.

John *starts to exit.*

Rai What about the bottles of champagne?

John I thought I'd stick them in a bath of cold water to keep them cool. I'll bring them down after dinner. Come on.

John *exits followed by* **Rai**, *leaving the stage empty as 'Rudolph' continues to play. After a couple of lines, the needle becomes stuck and the line 'You would even say it glows' is repeated over and over again. Eventually,* **Edie** *appears down the stairs laden with presents. She looks harrassed and exasperated.*

Edie Would no one else think of doing something about the record player, no?

Sean *comes hurrying in on stage left in an apron and a comic-looking white chef's hat.*

Sean Sorry, love – I was busy with the gravy.

Edie *pulls up the needle on the record player roughly. The music comes to an abrupt halt with a nasty-sounding scratch.* **Sean** *winces, but says nothing.*

Edie It was only a lot of old noise, anyway. I don't know who put it on. (*She looks up at* **Sean**) Why are you wearing that silly hat?

Sean It's my chef's hat. For doing the gravy.

Edie It looks daft.

Sean It's only a bit of fun, love.

Edie I'm sorry, Sean. Ignore me. It was just the noise of that record blaring in my ears, and the needle getting stuck and …

A beat. **Edie** *crosses to the Christmas tree and starts putting her presents under it.* **Sean** *watches her carefully.*

Sean Are you all right?

Edie I'm fine. Although I must say, I'm very disappointed the way it's turned out. (**Sean** *looks at her*) The weather. I really did think we had a chance of having a white Christmas. Not this … horrible rain.

Sean Maybe we'll get a white New Year.

Edie Maybe.

A pause. **Sean** *watches* **Edie** *intently as she gets up and begins to pull the table into place for Christmas dinner.*

Edie Give us a hand, will you?

Sean *does so. A pause as they manoeuvre the table into place. At length* **Edie** *speaks.*

Edie Do you think he still wants to exchange presents and … you know, join in the celebrations?

Sean I'm sure he does. It wouldn't be like John to make things awkward. I'm sure it's just … well, just the religious side of things he won't be joining in.

Edie (*acid*) Oh, well, that's all right, then. As long as he still believes in the eating and the drinking and the gluttony. And there was me thinking he'd gone to seed altogether.

A silence. **Edie** *continues setting the table.*

Sean (*eventually*) It's not the end of the world, you know. It's only his religion he's changed. He's still the same John.

Edie Yes.

A pause.

Sean And as long as he's not ramming it down our gullets – which he doesn't seem to be. That'd be the thing that'd worry me. If he became some class of a … of a converter or something. Some kind of proselytising whatd'youcallit. Like a Jehovah's Witness or something, always quoting the Buddhist bible at us. That's what'd drive me scatty. (*A beat*) Do Buddhists have a bible, do you know?

Edie   I've no idea.

Edward *enters.*

Sean   Edward'll know. (*To* **Edward**) Do you know do Buddhists have a bible?

Edie   As far as I can tell they have thousands. Buddhist monks spend donkey's years studying the scriptures.

Sean   Sure, I suppose all religions have to have some class of a … of a holy book or a book of rules or whatnot.

Edward   You make it sound like a particularly complicated version of golf.

Tara (*off*)   Dad!

Sean   My gravy!

And he darts off stage left. **DJ** *enters from upstairs.*

DJ   Cool, yous are up, can we do the presents now?

Edie   No, we cannot.

DJ   Why not?

Edie   Because I'm just about to serve dinner.

DJ But you've only just got up. How can we be just about to have dinner when you've only just got up? Turkeys take forever to cook.

Edie Is that so? Thank you for those words of wisom, Delia. (*A beat*) Tara's done most of it. With Edward.

DJ How come you got up so late, anyway? You've practically missed the whole of Christmas.

Edie I wasn't feeling well.

DJ What's wrong with you?

Sean Nothing you need worry your head about.

DJ Is it because John's become a Buddhist and he hates Christmas?

Sean He doesn't hate Christmas.

DJ Well, is it because he's become a Buddhist then?

Edie What John does is his own business, Julian. He's a big boy now.

DJ What is it, then?

Sean Look, Julian, go in and give Tara a hand like a good man, will you?

*This is evidently **Sean**'s final word on the subject, because he sits heavily in an armchair and picks up his newspaper.*

DJ Can we not do the presents before dinner?

Edie No, we cannot.

DJ Why not?

Edward We don't want to rush the presents, DJ. We want to take our time over them. I want to really savour this year's Car Boot Sale Special.

DJ Get lost!

Edie Julian, it's Christmas Day. Everybody just wants to relax. We'll give the presents out later. It'll give you something to look forward to for the rest of the day.

DJ I don't want something to look forward to. I want to do the presents.

Edie Well, you'll just have to wait until this evening.

DJ Why?

Edie You know very well why. Because we always give out our presents in the evening.

DJ For absolutely no reason.

Edie There is a reason.

DJ What is it then?

Edie Sean, you tell him. He won't listen to me.

Sean What's that?

Edie He wants to know why we always give out our presents in the evening and not in the morning.

Sean Oh. (*A beat. Then, to* **Edie**) Why do we always give out our presents in the evening and not in the morning?

Edie Because that's what we've always done. Because it's the tradition.

Sean There you go, Jules. Because it's tradition. That's as good a reason as any other.

DJ (*contemptuous*) Tradition!

Edie Yes, tradition. And if you've any complaints, you can go up there to the graveyard and complain to your dead grandfather, because it was him who invented the tradition.

DJ It's not fair.

Sean What's not fair about it?

DJ I'm the youngest so I never get to make up the traditions. I just get saddled with a whole load of boring ones left over from eight hundred years ago.

Edward Eight hundred years of oppression, hah, DJ?

At that moment **Tara** *comes through from the kitchen with a tray of condiments.*

The Buddhist of Castleknock

Tara That's life at the bottom of the evolutionary pile, I'm afraid, Jules.

Edward That's no way to refer to this proud country of ours!

Tara Get up there and give us a hand. That'd be more in your line now than sitting back dispensing witticisms and cynicisms.

And she exits to the kitchen again.

Edward Here, I've an idea. How about Julian gets to invent a tradition this year to be followed every year hence. What do you think of that, DJ?

Edie Edward ...

Sean No, hold on a minute, Edie. Traditions have to start somewhere. If Julian can come up with a new tradition, the least we could all do is follow it.

Edward Assuming it's legal and at least reasonably tasteful.

Sean Absolutely. Julian?

DJ OK. I hereby invent the tradition that presents are given out as soon as everybody gets up on Christmas Day.

Sean Uh-uh. Sorry.

DJ What?

Sean It can't be a tradition that conflicts with an existing tradition. Existing traditions take precedence.

DJ But the whole of Christmas is just one boring old tradition after another! There's no room for any new ones!

Sean You'll just have to be creative.

DJ *sighs and shakes his head. He crosses to the Christmas tree and starts to rummage through the presents piled underneath.*

DJ Which one's mine?

Edie Get away – shoo! Never mind which one is yours.

DJ Mum, it's Christmas Day! If I can't open my present until this evening, the least you could do is let me see it.

Edie No – you'll guess what it is.

DJ That's part of the fun!

Edie Ah, Julian, could you not wait until—

DJ (*shaking a parcel*) Is this mine?

Edie Julian!

DJ Is it?

Edie Sean, tell him—

Sean Julian! Put that present down now!

DJ It *is* mine, isn't it?

The Buddhist of Castleknock

Edie Julian!

DJ For fuck's sake!

And he throws the present down violently and storms out into the hall and off up the stairs.

Edie Julian!

But he's gone. A silence.

Edie What was that about?

Tara I think he was hoping for a motorised scooter.

Edie Pity about him. Do you know what those things cost?

Tara You should have asked me. I could have chipped in.

Edward We all could have.

Edie It's not a question of money. He needs to learn – you don't just get everything you want the moment you want it. He's getting far too materialistic, that boy.

Edward Steady on there, Mum – you're starting to sound like a Buddhist!

Edie (*cold*) Spirituality and values aren't exclusive to Buddhists, Edward. Whatever your brother might think.

Edward I don't think John would claim—

Edie Ssh! What's that?

Edward What?

Edie Can you hear that?

Tara Hear what?

Edie That. It's like a mooing sound. Listen.

Sean *crosses to the foot of the stairs and listens too. And from upstairs we too hear a very faint moaning sound.*

Edie Do you hear it?

Sean It's coming from Rai's room.

Tara My room.

Edie They're up to something. I'm going up to put a stop to it.

Edward Mum, it's Christmas.

Edie And?

Edward And they've been sleeping in separate rooms.

Edie So?

Edward So I would imagine they're …

Edie What?

Edward Well, you know ... what young Buddhist men and women do ... together. In a bedroom.

Edie What's that?

Edward You know ...

He raises his eyebrows suggestively. The others look at him.

Edward Oh for God's sake – chanting – meditating. It's what Buddhists do, isn't it?

Edie Right, that's it.

Sean Edie ...

Edie Sean, it is not natural. This is my house, and I will not have strange religious chanting going on in it.

Edward The rosary excepted.

Edie And if you don't like it, you can convert to being a Buddhist too!

Sean Edie, love, do you not think you're overreacting slightly to this whole thing?

Edie No, Sean, I don't. On the contrary, I think I have been remarkably patient and tolerant. When John told me he wanted to bring some girl he's only just met into our house for Christmas, I welcomed her into the bosom of our family. And when Rai turned out to be ... who she was, I didn't bat an eyelid, unlike some I could mention. And I've tolerated John announcing out of the blue that the Catholic faith is a pile of old codswollop. But I will not have him ruin Christmas for everybody by turning my house into a Buddhist temple! I just will not have it, Sean!

Edie *is close to tears now.* **Sean** *looks at* **Edward** *and* **Tara** *and motions for them to leave him and* **Edie** *alone.* **Tara** *and* **Edward** *exit in the direction of the kitchen. A beat.*

Sean Edie, I don't like John becoming a bloody Buddhist any more than you do. But what can we do about it? It's his life.

Edie I think you should talk to him. Find out if anything's wrong. (**Sean** *looks sceptical*) I'm worried about him, Sean. I'm afraid he's unhappy. John wouldn't do something like this unless he was unhappy. Unless he was searching for something.

Sean Aren't we all searching for something?

Edie You don't just cast off your whole background and heritage and … culture like that unless you're missing something … fundamental inside.

Sean Like what?

Edie I don't know. Something he should have had as a child. Something we should have given him.

Sean Everyone has to find their own way, Edie. That's all he's doing. Trying to find his own way.

Edie What's wrong with the way we've given him? It's served us all right, hasn't it?

The Buddhist of Castleknock

Sean It's no reflection on us that John's experimenting with other ways.

Edie Maybe you're right. Maybe it's just a phase. I mean, he's only been a Buddhist about five minutes. Sure, he's like someone who hasn't even made his Holy Communion yet.

Sean Exactly. This time next year he'll probably be in here saying the rosary with the best of us.

Edie I think you should talk to him all the same.

Sean What do you want me to say to him?

Edie Find out if he's planning to join in the Christmas celebrations, for a start.

Sean He said he was, didn't he?

Edie He said he wasn't going to let it spoil Christmas for everybody else. That isn't the same thing. I mean, we don't even know if he's still called John, for Heaven's sake!

Sean What else would he be called?

Edie Well, these Buddhists – don't they take strange religious names when they convert? Mustapha or Haseem or …

Sean Mustapha Sullivan. You've got to say, it has a certain ring to it.

Edie It's not funny, Sean.

Sean Look, if John was going to change his name, I'm sure he'd have told us by now.

Edie He's probably a vegetarian too. You can't believe in reincarnation and then go around eating animals. You could end up eating your own grandmother. What am I going to feed him for Christmas dinner if he doesn't eat meat any more?

Sean Can't he just leave the turkey and the ham and eat the rest?

Edie Ah, don't be ridiculous – he can't just eat Brussels sprouts and stuffing for his Christmas dinner!

Sean Edie …

Edie Sean, our son is clearly deeply unhappy! So unhappy that he's joined a different religious faith. If we don't want to lose him altogether, I think one of us needs to talk to him. And you're his father, he'll listen to you.

At that moment, **John** *appears with* **Rai**.

John Mum, you're up – Happy Christmas!

Edie Happy Christmas, love.

Rai Merry Christmas, Mrs Sullivan.

Edie Merry Christmas, Rai, love. (*A beat*) I wasn't sure if you people said that. Buddhists, I mean, not …

Rai When in Rome …

Edie Of course.

John How was midnight mass?

Edie Very nice, thank you.

John Father Aidan's sermon didn't go on too long? (*To* **Rai**) Honest to God, Rai – sometimes you'd swear that man was on a sponsored sermon, getting paid by the minute.

Edie (*a little terser than necessary*) Father Aidan gave a lovely sermon. Didn't he, Sean?

Sean He certainly did. (*To* **Rai**) Though I have to admit, it wasn't the shortest sermon I've heard.

Edie It *is* Christmas, Sean. The centrepiece of the Christian calendar.

Sean I suppose it is …

Edward *appears back from the kitchen.* **Edie** *spots him, and springs into action.*

Edie Rai, love, why don't you come and give Tara and myself a hand finishing off the dinner?

Rai Sure.

Edie And Edward – if you want to get your presents under the tree before dinner, you'd better get wrapping; we'll be eating in less than a quarter of an hour.

Edward Righto. (*To* **Rai**) Daren't risk the wrath of DJ a second time.

Rai *laughs.* **Edward** *exits up the stairs to wrap his presents.*

Edie Come on, Rai, love. Let's get these vegetables on the go.

And she ushers **Rai** *out towards the kitchen. A pause.* **John** *goes to pick up a magazine.*

Sean John?

John *stops and turns to look at* **Sean***.*

Sean I just wondered, you know … before dinner … if we could have a little chat. Just the two of us.

John What about?

A pause. **John** *looks at* **Sean***.* **Sean** *fiddles with a pipe and a tin of tobacco which he takes from his inside pocket.*

Sean (*uneasy*) It's hard, this, John, you know? For your mother especially.

John You don't approve?

Sean It's not a question of approving or disapproving. It's more a question of trying to understand.

John Is it Rai you don't approve of?

Sean God no, it's not Rai … Lord, your mother would hate you to think …

John So it's the Buddhist thing?

Sean The Buddhist thing ... yes. It's the religion thing that your mother ... that we find ...

John Difficult?

Sean (*nods*) To understand.

John There isn't much to say, Dad. It isn't a big deal.

Sean Ah well, now, it *is* a big deal, John. Otherwise you wouldn't have done it. You'd have stayed a Catholic and just ... you know ... stopped going to mass and that, d'you know?

John Like the others did?

Sean This is it.

A silence.

Sean It isn't every day you come across the fella who tells his parents on Christmas Eve that he's become a Buddhist monk, d'you know.

John Not a monk. Just a Buddhist.

Sean All the same. It'd be a worry. To your mother, especially.

John There's nothing to worry about, Da. It's just a different path. To the same end.

Sean We're all going to die right enough.

John So there's nothing to get worked up about.

A pause.

Sean Still and all, these kinds of strange beliefs, d'you know? They'd be inclined to frighten your mother a bit.

John Afraid I'll come back as a tree?

Sean Ah no, it'd be more—

John Afraid you'll come back as a tree?

Sean (*exasperated*) Ah John, will you stop! Your mother's worried about you. She thinks there's something troubling you. Is it maybe money, like? Because we could help you out if—

John It's not money, Da.

Sean Or Rai, she's not—

John (*with a smile*) Black? Oh she is, Dad. She's definitely black, I'm afraid.

Sean I meant is she … you know …

John She's not pregnant, no. (*A beat*) Not as far as I'm aware, anyway.

Sean *nods. A pause.*

Sean So …

The Buddhist of Castleknock

John So what?

Sean Ach, John, you're making this awful hard. I'm trying to talk to you and ... and trying to find out a bit about the whole thing that I can tell your mother and you're not making it one bit easy.

John What do you want to know?

Sean Your mother wants to know if you're planning on giving out presents, for a start.

John Of course. It's Christmas, isn't it?

Sean That's what I said.

John Well, there you go then.

Sean And she wants to know ... what it is you're looking for. With the Buddhist bit, like.

John I don't know the answer to that, Da. But the fun is in the looking, isn't it?

Sean *nods. A pause. At length,* **Sean** *breaks the silence.*

Sean You know, I remember one Friday night way back in the sixties sitting down there with the mother and the father one night at home in Athlone to watch the *Late Late Show* on the television. I couldn't have been much younger than you are now, and I had a job working in O'Malley's insurance firm in the town. A good job – nice, steady income – but I was getting restless, d'you know? Anxious to see other things, maybe move up to Dublin or what have you, maybe see a bit of the world. Anyways, we sat down that night, your granny, your grandad and me, and they had a young fellow from Trinity College on to talk about drama, or writing or some such. And what did he do, only instead of talking about drama, he started criticising the Church, and he called one of the archbishops a moron. On the telly now, like. A moron. Brazen as you like. And there was uproar. I remember my father saying he should be thrown out of the college for daring to speak of a member of God's holy clergy like that. A young pup, my father called him. An ungrateful young pup. And your granny over in the corner nodding like her head was going to fall off. But inside I was cheering the young pup. Urging him on. And the next week he came back on and apologised, and then what did he do, only straight away he said the archbishop knew what the word 'moron' meant, but did he know the meaning of the word 'Christianity'? Well, it was all over the next day's papers. And I remember reading the whole thing with a horrified sense of … liberation. Like some class of a dam had burst open inside me, inside the whole country. And I resolved to pack in the job in O'Malleys and go off to Paris, or Prague, or Bucharest, and grow a beard and wear sandals, and read Mao and live in a hippie commune and …

Sean *breaks off. A long pause.*

John   And then?

Sean   And then three weeks later I met your mother. And we got married, and had Tara. And I don't regret a single moment of it. But it's not so easy to sit cross-legged in a tent trying to work out the meaning of life when you've a family to support.

John *nods, and one senses a moment of communion between father and son.*

Sean Still and all, at least we made it up to Dublin eventually, wha'?

John And you grew the beard.

Sean That too.

A beat.

Sean There's no shame in being happy with your lot, John.

John I know.

Sean There'd be some fellows, now, would always be looking for something else. Never taking the time to stand still and enjoy the view from the top of the mountain, or halfway up the mountain, or wherever it is they've got to. They'd always be racing to get to the next corner to see if the view was better from there. D'you know? There's no shame in standing a while to admire the view.

John No.

Sean And sure, isn't that the whole point of being a Buddhist, as I understand it? Accepting your lot with – what's the word? … 'equanimity', and doing your best to enjoy it.

John That's as good a definition of the Four Noble Truths as any, I suppose. (*He looks up at* **Sean**) The Four Noble truths – the core of Buddhist teaching.

Sean Well, there you have it.

A pause.

John I'm not unhappy, Da. I promise you. You can tell Mum – I'm not unhappy.

Sean *nods. A pause.*

John But maybe I am … I don't know … scared of being happy.

Sean Why in the name of God would anyone be scared of being happy?

John Because once you're happy – once you reach the point in your life where you can stop and look around and admire the view and say 'I am truly happy now' – then you stop growing, don't you? You atrophy.

Sean Why do you?

John Because you stop *wanting* to grow. You stop wanting to change. Or learn. Or seek new experiences. You just want everything to stay the way it is. You don't want anything to change ever again, so you can just remain in that intoxicating state of bliss forever. And eventually the brief moment of happiness evaporates. But not before a giant barbed wire fence has been built around your life. Because once you've glimpsed happiness once, you're condemned to spending the rest of your life in the same tiny field of experience, trying to repeat the unrepeatable. To starting back down the hill again, retracing your steps in search of some past contentment you think you had rather than forging ahead and seeking out new experiences.

Sean And that's why you've become a Buddhist?

John I don't know why I've become a Buddhist, Da. I just know that right now, it suits me.

Sean *nods. A pause.*

Sean So ... do you think your mother and I have stopped living because we're ... content?

John Do you?

Sean I don't know, John. I honestly don't know. But you're right about one thing. The excitement's in the chase all right. The moving and the searching and the seeking out new experiences – that's all well and good. The trick is knowing when to stop. The trick is knowing when you've found what you were looking for.

Before **John** *can reply,* **Edward** *comes down the stairs with an armful of presents.*

Edward Right, that's the presents done – how are we doing for dinner?

And he crosses to put his presents under the tree.

John I'd better go and see if they need a hand in the kitchen.

And he makes to exit stage right.

Sean John? (**John** *turns back*) One other thing.

John What's that?

Sean You're still called John, aren't you? Your mother's worried you'll have changed your name so you're called after some Eastern prophet or the like.

John Now that you mention it, my Buddhist name is Pema Temsin Wang Po – Ocean of the Lotus Teaching. But you can call me Temsin for short.

Sean (*horrified*) No …?!

John (*with a wink*) Don't worry, Da. I'm still John to close friends and family …

At that moment **Edie** *and* **Rai** *enter stage right, carrying dishes of steaming vegetables, plates of turkey already carved, etc. etc.*

Rai No, please – we can manage fine. You lot stay where you are.

Edie (*indulgent, with a faint air of forced jollity*) Awful, aren't they, Rai? I always say, for everything women's lib has achieved, at Christmas, everything somehow always reverts back to type. The women serve the dinner, the men carve the turkey.

Sean I made the stuffing.

Edward And I did most of the vegetables.

Edie (*ignoring them*) Do the men in your house do the same?

Rai They wouldn't dare. Or they'd have me to deal with.

Edie Well, good for you. Though I think maybe it's partly my fault in this house. I think maybe I spoil my men a bit.

'My men' – isn't that a gas way to think of them now, altogether? As if they're were all my husbands?

Rai You want to get them up off their fat backsides to give you a hand, Mrs Sullivan.

Edie Ach, well, I don't mind doing it. Sure, doesn't it keep me off the streets and out of mischief?

Rai I tell you something – I wouldn't stand for it. John!

John's *away in a world of his own. He looks up, a little startled.*

Rai Come and give your mother a hand.

John Sorry. What do you want me to do?

Edie I think we're nearly there now.

John There must be something I can do.

Edie Honestly, love, you just sit down there and relax. We can manage. (*To* **Rai**) Can't we, love? (*She continues without waiting for an answer*) Sure, it's practically all done. But thanks for offering, love. It's very considerate of you.

At that moment, **Tara** *appears with the final plate of food.*

Tara That's the lot, folks. Come and get it.

Edie Right. You can all come and sit down now. Someone call Julian. (**Edward** *crosses towards the hall to call* **DJ**) Rai, love, I've put you next to Tara. Keep the girls together where we can do the most mischief!

Edward (*calling upstairs*)   DJ! Dinner's ready. So stop pulling your wire and come on down and pull a cracker instead.

Edie   Edward!

Edward   Sorry.

DJ (*appearing from the hall*)   I want to sit at the end where I can see the telly.

Edie   You needn't bother, Julian – we're not having the television on during Christmas dinner.

DJ   Why not?

Edie   Because we're having our Christmas dinner, Julian. Together. As a family. And we don't want the television blaring in the background.

DJ   *You* don't, you mean. No one else minds.

Edie   Julian, I'm not going to argue with you. Rai, will you have a glass of wine?

Rai   No, thank you.

Sean   Ah, go on, you'll have one – it's Christmas Day.

Rai   Honestly, I'm fine. We … I don't drink.

Tara   Not even at Christmas?

Rai   No. Thank you. (*Awkward, not wishing to offend*) It's …

one of the things about being a Buddhist. You're meant to try and abstain from intoxicants of the mind.

Tara Well, you can make mine a large one, Dad.

Sean *pours* **Tara** *a large glass of wine.*

John It's not written in stone … not like the Ten Commandments. But … well, if you can, like …

By this stage **Sean** *has moved on to where* **John** *is sitting.*

Sean You're not off it too, are you, John?

John Well, I—

Tara Ah, for the love of God, John, it's Christmas Day.

Edward You're not serious?

John 'Fraid so.

Tara Didn't I see you wandering around this morning carrying two enormous bottles of champagne?

John That was for the rest of you. As a gesture.

Tara (*dry*) How considerate of you.

Sean Lord God, thank goodness we've none of that kind of nonsense with Catholicism. Catholicism is founded on intoxication.

Edie It's founded on the body and blood of Christ, Sean. It's not the same.

Sean Either way – thanks be to the Divine Jaysus Ireland isn't a Buddhist country. (*To* **John**) You won't even have a drop, so? For the Christmas?

A beat, as **John** *wavers.*

John Go on, so – I suppose a little drop wouldn't hurt.

Sean Good lad yourself.

John *holds out his glass and* **Sean** *pours him a glass of wine.*

John (*to* **Rai**) It's just a drop. For Christmas.

Rai Don't look at me, mate. You do what you like.

Sean *sits back into his chair and raises his glass in a toast.*

Sean Happy Christmas, everybody!

All Happy Christmas!

And they clink glasses, etc. A pause, as they set about serving themselves, passing vegetables over and back, etc.

John I have to admit – giving up the drink has been the hardest bit of the whole thing for me.

Sean I can imagine.

The Buddhist of Castleknock

Edward Gas, isn't it? He doesn't mind the fact that he might come back as a tadpole, but tell him he'll never enjoy another creamy pint of stout …

Tara So does this mean you'll go to Buddhist hell? Because you broke the pledge?

Rai Buddhists don't really have a hell.

John Or a pledge.

Tara What do they have?

Rai The *samsara* – it's like the endless cycle of birth and rebirth.

Tara And that's the Buddhist concept of hell – living forever?

Rai That's right – coming back time and time again to undergo the pain and suffering of life.

Tara Sounds great to me. Doesn't it sound great to you, Mum?

Edie I don't know. I'd be very suspicious of anything like that.

Edie *trails off uncertainly. She's out of her depth here. A beat.*

Sean What's the alternative? To constant reincarnation?

John Nirvana.

Tara Buddhist heaven.

John Except nirvana is more like a state of mind. You can even reach it during this life. You know, through meditation and that.

Sean And that's why those Buddhist monks spend their days up there in their caves in the Himalayas chanting and meditating?

John Trying to cleanse the mind and reach nirvana.

Edward So what's the difference when you die?

Rai When you die you reach paranirvana.

John A kind of permanent state of nirvana. Peace. Enlightenment.

Sean Well, I don't know about anyone else, but I intend to reach an impermanent state of nirvana right now by drinking myself under the table. Edward?

Edward (*holding out his glass*) Fill her up.

Sean *does so, then gets up and goes to get another bottle of wine.*

DJ (*to* **Rai**) Do you mind the telly being on during dinner?

Rai Doesn't bother me, mate – telly's always on in our house.

DJ See?

Edie Julian, I'm not discussing it any further.

DJ But the *Only Fools and Horses Christmas Special* is on!

Edward DJ, they've had the same *Only Fools and Horses Christmas Special* on for the past four years.

DJ (*triumphant*) Exactly! It's a Christmas tradition!

Sean Julian, stop being silly, and pass me over your mother's glass there.

DJ (*ignoring him*) The *Only Fools and Horses Christmas Special* is as much a Christmas tradition as putting Mammy's Angel on the tree and 'Away in Some Bloody Manger'! How come I have to follow all of your traditions, and I don't get to follow any of mine?

Edie Because our traditions aren't rude and anti-social. Our traditions are about community, about doing things together, as a family.

DJ Stupid things.

Edie You might think so. We don't. Isn't that right, Rai?

Rai I have to admit, I'm kind of a fan of *Only Fools and Horses*. So I can see your point, DJ.

Edie (*dry*) Can you indeed? Brussel sprouts?

Rai No thanks. I'm not all that gone on Brussels sprouts.

Tara (*sotto voce – but not sotto voce enough*) Oh, excuse me, Miss-Fan-of-*Only-Fools-and-Horses*-Doesn't-Like-Brussels-Sprouts!

Jim O'Hanlon

Sean Tara!

Tara Well, I'm sorry, but—

Edie All right, everybody, that'll do. We are not turning on the television, and that's the end of it.

Rai I wasn't suggesting we turn it on. I just, you know, I just enjoy watching it, you know?

An awkward silence as they eat – the only sound the clinking of cutlery. After a long pause, **DJ** *breaks the silence.*

DJ We could watch *Only Fools and Horses* together – (*mimics* Edie) 'as a family'.

Edie (*losing her temper*) Julian! That is enough! If there's any more out of you you'll get no Christmas dinner, no *Fools or Horses* and no flipping present, either! Now just stop it!

A silence, as they all look at **Edie** *in amazement.*

Edie (*calming herself*) Rai, love, help yourself to vegetables, before they get cold.

Rai Thank you.

John Pass us over your wine glass there, DJ.

DJ *does so.*

Sean I see you didn't need to be asked twice if you wanted a glass of wine.

John (*pouring* **DJ** *a glass of wine*) Sure, you can always tape *Only Fools and Horses*.

Edie John!

John What?

Edie He's only fifteen.

John *Only Fools and Horses* isn't over fifteens, is it?

Edie I meant …

She nods in the direction of the wine.

John What?

Edie The wine, John. He's too young to drink.

DJ Mum!

Edie Julian, I don't want to hear it. You're only fifteen, you're not having wine. End of story.

Edward He's fifteen, Mum. He's probably been getting blow jobs down the park since he was twelve.

Edie and **Sean** (*together*) Edward!

Tara Edward's right, Mum. Julian's not going to get—

Edie Tara, I really don't think you're in a position to be giving advice on drinking, do you?

A silence.

Edie I'm sorry, I didn't mean ...

Tara That's all right.

Edie Tara, love.

Tara Honestly, Mum, it's fine. Pass me over the cranberry sauce there, would you, Edward?

A beat, as **John** *passes her the cranberry sauce.*

Edie Who's for Brussels sprouts? John?

John No thanks.

Edie No?

John I'm not a big fan, either.

Edie You've always eaten them before.

John I know. But only a couple. And only for the sake of tradition.

Edie I always thought you liked Brussels sprouts.

John *shakes his head.*

Tara I never knew you didn't like Brussels sprouts either.

John I'm sorry, I didn't realise you required a personal press release.

The Buddhist of Castleknock

Tara Did you know John didn't like Brussels sprouts, Edward?

Edward Yes.

Edie You did? How come you never said?

Edward What difference would it have made?

Edie I wouldn't have made so many, for a start. If I'd known Rai didn't like them, and neither does John.

Tara Is that part of the Buddhist law too? No Brussels sprouts?

Edie Tara!

DJ I hate Brussels sprouts.

Edie Well, I know that. You hate anything that doesn't contain at least seventy E numbers.

DJ No. I just hate Brussels sprouts, that's all.

Edie And cabbage. And carrots. And courgettes, and—

Sean (*quickly*) Well, I love Brussels sprouts. Rai, you'd never pass them over there, would you?

Rai Sure.

Edie What am I going to do with all the leftover Brussels sprouts?

Edward Brussel sprout soup?

Rai Brussels curry?

Edward Brothel Sprouts?

A beat. The others look at him.

Edward A prostitute's baby. A brothel sprout.

Edie Edward!

Tara You might have told us before I spent an hour and a half cleaning two hundred of the bloody things this morning.

John What the fuck business is it of yours whether I eat Brussels fucking sprouts or I don't?

Edie Look, it doesn't matter—

DJ How come he's allowed to swear and I'm not?

Edie John, don't swear at the dinner table, please.

DJ Oh, but he can swear anywhere else?

Sean Julian, put a sock in it.

Tara Don't go taking it out on me, John.

John Taking what out on you? What are you talking about, Tara?

Sean Here, DJ – how about pulling an oul' cracker there?

He proffers a cracker. **Edward** *gets up and heads into the kitchen with a bowl to get more vegetables.*

Tara It isn't my fault you've become so po-faced you can't even enjoy Christmas any more.

Meanwhile, **DJ***'s pulled the cracker and won.*

Sean Good man yourself. What have you won?

DJ What do you think I've won? A gay hat and a crap joke.

Edie Julian!

DJ Well, why can't I watch—

Edie If I hear another word out of you about the television—

John (*quietly*) Take that back, Tara.

Tara Take what back?

John What you said about me and Rai just now. Take it back.

Tara I never said anything about Rai. I said you were too po-faced—

John I'm warning you, Tara.

Edie Tara, apologise to your brother.

Tara He said so himself, Mum. He's a Buddhist now, so he doesn't want to celebrate Christmas any more. Dad, pass me the wine.

Sean Tara, love …

Tara Do I have to come and get it myself?

Edie Tara, are you sure?

Tara I'm an alcoholic, Mum. Remember? That's what alcoholics do. They drink. Now please, pass me the wine, Dad.

Edward (*returning with his bowl of vegetables*) Tara—

Tara Don't you start as well, Edward! Just because he (**John**) has poisoned the whole atmosphere. Julian, pass me the wine, please.

DJ You're such a lazy cow!

Edie Julian! Don't speak to your sister like that!

DJ She is, though! She's a fat, lazy cow!

Tara I've actually lost weight, I'll have you know!

DJ You mean you were even fatter before? No wonder you became an alcoholic!

Edie Julian!

Tara The one time of the year we can all get together as a family! The one time of the year we get a chance to be happy—

Edward Well, I don't know about anybody else, but I'm having the time of my life – DJ?

DJ I would be if I could watch—

Edie Don't you dare mention that confounded programme!

John (*very quiet, to* **Tara**) Take that back.

Tara No.

John Take it back.

Tara I will not! It was you—

Tara *pulls up abruptly and touches her forehead. She looks up at the ceiling.*

Tara What was that?

Sean What?

Tara I just felt a … there's another.

Edie Another what?

John It felt like a drop of water.

Edward (*facetious*) Probably just storm clouds gathering …

Edie How can it be … ? Who used the bath last?

John I put the champagne into a bath of water to keep it cold. Why?

Edie Jesus, Mary and Joseph – the tap!

Edward I'll go!

Sean Quick, Edward – before the ceiling comes in on top of us!

Edward *and* **Sean** *run up the stairs.*

John What tap?

Edie The tap in the bathroom – it doesn't close properly!

John But I turned it—

Edie You mustn't have done it properly! The bath'll have overflowed!

John *stares at* **Edie** *in a state of paralysed horror.*

Tara (*pouring herself another glass of wine*) Congratulations, John – you've finally managed it!

John How was I to know there was something wrong with the bloody tap? How was I supposed to *divine* that—

Edie John, that is enough! We've just about had our fill of your carry on this Christmas!

John What have I done?

Edie 'What have I done?' 'What have I done?', he says! I'll tell you what you've done. I'll tell you what you're doing! You're ruining Christmas! You're ruining it for everybody!

Edie *shouts and brings her fist down on the table with a tremendous thud, just as* **Edward** *comes running down the stairs. There is a brief, stunned silence, followed by a gentle creaking sound.* **Sean** *turns just as the Christmas tree starts to topple.*

Sean   Look out!

The Christmas tree falls over with a crash. Almost at the same moment, there is another creaking sound from above and the ceiling gives way under the weight of the flooding in the bathroom, sending a cascade of plaster and water onto the middle of the dinner table. The whole thing is over in a couple of seconds, leaving them all drenched and covered in plaster from the ceiling. A beat as they all sit in horrified silence.

DJ (*eventually, turning on the television*)   I told you that tree was lopsided.

Blackout.

Act Two

Scene Two

It is later on Christmas night. The dinner has been cleared away, as has the plaster from the ceiling. As the lights come up, **DJ** *and* **Tara** *are putting the Christmas tree back up.* **Tara** *stands back from the tree issuing instructions. On the other side of the room,* **Sean** *is reading a book on basic Buddhism, watched by* **Rai** *and* **John**.

Tara Right, left a bit. Left!

DJ You said 'right'.

Tara I said 'right' as in 'all right'. It needs to go left.

DJ For fuck's sake!

Tara OK, hold it a bit more towards me now. (*He does so*) That's it. Right, Jules, if you can keep it there now. That's it. Perfect.

DJ *emerges from the branches at the foot of the Christmas tree.*

Tara You know something? Now that I see it like that, I think you're right – it was lopsided before.

Edward It certainly isn't lopsided now.

Rai What do you think, Mr Sullivan? Could you be tempted?

Sean There's an awful lot of numbers and lists. (*reads*) 'The Four Noble Truths, the Noble Eightfold Path, the Three Marks of Conditioned Existence' – give me the Our Father and the Glory Be any day. Much less complicated.

Rai It's not so bad once you get your head around it. A lot of it is self-evident.

John And a lot of it corresponds to what Catholicism teaches if you dig deep enough.

Rai If you could get beyond the layers of hierarchy and social teaching.

Edward You mean if it wasn't Catholicism.

Sean And you really meditate? For real?

John Of course.

Sean Ye weren't just doing it to wind your mother up?

John Of course not.

Sean Well, rather you than me is all I can say.

Rai So we can't seduce you into converting?

Sean Can you imagine what Jimmy and Kathleen would say?

Edward Don't mind Jimmy and Kathleen – imagine what Mum would say!

Tara (*pouring herself a drink*) Quite right, too. Load of old nonsense.

DJ Do you think if I became a Buddhist I could come back as a Premiership striker?

Edward You might. But you wouldn't be allowed to drink.

DJ Oh yeah. (*A beat*) Ah well, fuck that, so.

Sean Julian.

DJ What? Mum's in bed.

Sean It's got nothing to do with Mum. I don't want swearing in the house either.

DJ For God's sake!

Rai She's been asleep for hours. Do you think she's all right?

Sean I'm sure she's grand. She probably just got a bit of a shock.

John Maybe you should go and check on her. Just to be sure.

Sean Ach, I'm sure she's grand.

Tara She's going to miss the whole of Christmas.

Sean Well – maybe I'll see does she feel like coming down for a game of cards or something. Tara, do you want to get the cards, and we'll see if we can get an oul' game going?

Sean *gets up and crosses towards the stairs.* **Tara** *goes to the dresser and rummages in a drawer for a pack of cards.*

The Buddhist of Castleknock

Tara Is it any wonder she's in shock when himself comes home and tells her he's a Buddhist on Christmas Eve. You couldn't have picked a more appropriate time to tell her, no?

John I wanted to tell her face to face. This was the first chance I had.

DJ It's not just that. She's been acting really weird for weeks. Always bursting into tears if I do the slightest thing.

Edward DJ, you'd drive a statue to tears. In fact, come to think of it, you weren't knocking around Ballinaspittle sometime in the early eighties, were you?

DJ Ha ha! Right, I'm going out. I'll see yous later.

Sean reappears down the stairs.

Sean Jaysus, one day you ask him to spend with his family, one day of the year, and even that's too much for him.

Tara (*glaring at* **John**) Is it any wonder?

Sean Still sleeping like a baby, poor love. She's been under a lot of pressure lately. Getting ready for Christmas and that.

Rai She wants to try some meditation.

Tara (*snorts*) Meditation!

John It's really good, Tara. Really relaxes you.

Tara I've enough to worry about without getting into bloody meditation.

Rai You don't fancy giving it a go, then?

Tara No. Thank you.

Rai Mr Sullivan?

Sean I don't think so, love. It's not really my ... cup of tea, you know?

Edward Go on, Da. You look like you could use a bit of relaxation.

Sean Ah no, I'm—

Edward He'd love to try it. And so would I.

Rai Mr Sullivan?

Sean *looks at her – he's had just about enough to drink to give it a go.*

Sean What do I have to do?

Rai Hey, fantastic!

Tara What about our game of cards?

Sean I thought we should wait for your mum to get up. She'd hate to miss out on the cards.

Rai This exercise only takes about ten minutes. You sure you don't want to try it, Tara?

Tara Thank you. I'll stick to vodka. Dad?

Sean No thanks, love. I don't think my body would tolerate any more alcohol.

Edward Besides, we're meditating.

Tara *crosses to the drinks cabinet and pours herself a vodka, then sits at the dining room table upstage right playing Patience with herself. Throughout the following,* **Tara** *alternates between playing Patience and keeping an eye on the proceedings.*

Rai Right. John and Edward and I can sit on these cushions. Mr Sullivan, you stay where you are.

Sean You mean I don't get to sit cross-legged on the floor? What kind of meditation is this?

Rai You can if you want. I just thought …

Sean A concession to the elder Buddhist, hah? I'm grand here.

John *and* **Rai** *arrange themselves cross-legged on the floor.*

Rai Right then. Edward – see the way John and I are sitting? You need to sit like that. And then you hold your hands on your lap like this, one inside the other, like a cup, thumbs touching. You too, Mr Sullivan. Just get your feet flat on the ground. That's it. Okay, now close your eyes, and just concentrate on your breathing.

Sean *and* **Edward** *do as bid.*

Rai Concentrate first of all on the breath as it goes into and then exits the body. On the sensation of it travelling down your nostrils into your lungs, and then being pushed up and out again. The idea is to focus your attention on your breathing so that you're completely aware of the present moment, completely focused on what's happening to you at this precise moment in time. That's what meditation is – being totally aware of what's happening to you as it's happening, no matter what it is.

Sean So we just concentrate on our breathing?

John That's right. When we do this exercise at the Buddhist centre in London, we say the phrase 'Um Ah Hung' at the end of each cycle of breaths.

Tara (*snorts*) You *are* joking?

Rai It's just a tool to keep you aware of your breathing. Like an anchor – something to fall back on if you lose your bearings. But you can just count, one, two, three – up to ten.

Edward Sure, we may as well say the 'Um Ah Hung' bit. Get the full experience, what do you think, Da?

Sean Sure, why not? As the fella says, we may as well be 'Um Ah Hung' for a sheep as a lamb.

John Well, if it doesn't make you feel uncomfortable …

Tara You mean more uncomfortable than sitting cross-legged on the floor with a gut full of turkey?

Rai Right then. 'Um Ah Hung' it is. After each out breath. Nice and gently.

They start to concentrate on their breathing and to say the phrase 'Um Ah Hung' on each cycle of breaths. This continues for a couple of seconds. **Tara** *watches all the while, vodka in hand.*

Sean I tell you – it isn't as easy as it looks.

Rai Keep concentrating. Just free your mind completely from everything except an awareness of your breathing.

She takes another breath, and on the out-breath, chants the phrase 'Um Ah Hung' as before. The others follow suit. **Sean** *starts to laugh gently.*

Sean I keep wondering what Jimmy would say if he could see me here. (*He opens his eyes and leans across to address* **Rai**) Jimmy's married to Edie's sister, Kathleen. We had a double wedding, like, and Jimmy is—

John Dad!

Sean Sorry.

Sean *closes his eyes again and goes back to concentrating on his breathing. A silence, broken only by the breathing of the four meditators and their chants of 'Um Ah Hung' after each cycle of breaths. At first, they chant the word at different times, but before long, their breathing patterns have synchronised, and they are chanting the phrase as a chorus.*

Sean (*eyes still closed*) Begod, d'you know – I think it's working. I feel great.

Tara That'll be the whiskey.

Sean No, fair's fair, credit where it's due, the breathing is—

John Dad!

Sean Sorry.

Again the sound of the meditators' breathing and intoning the phrase 'Um Ah Hung'. This goes on for some time. **Tara** *begins to look increasingly agitated. She turns away from the circle of meditators and pours herself another vodka, which she drinks in one go. She's about to pour herself another when* **Edie** *appears in her dressing gown.*

Edie Jesus, Mary and Joseph.

Sean *opens his eyes and jumps to his feet.*

Sean Edie, love. Did we wake you? We were just—

Edie Have you gone completely mad, Sean?

Sean It was only a bit of fun, love. John and Rai were just showing me a Buddhist relaxation technique. D'you know … to help me … relax, and that.

Edie I would remind you all that today is Christmas Day. If you can't relax on Christmas Day …

Tara Mum's right. It's the one day of the year you're meant to be able to relax without needing Buddhist meditation techniques.

The Buddhist of Castleknock

John It isn't a religious thing, Mum.

Edie I don't care what it is, John. I don't want it in my house. You've done enough damage for today, thank you very much.

John Mum—

Edie Not content with ruining our Christmas dinner, you have to start bringing hokum-pokum chanting and meditating into the house! Well, I won't have it, John! I think I've been very tolerant up to now! But I will not have my house turned into a Buddhist temple on Christmas Day!

Rai It's my fault, Mrs Sullivan. I'm sorry. I didn't mean to ruin your Christmas.

John You haven't ruined anything, Rai.

Tara Yes she has.

Edie Tara!

Tara Well, it's true. She's caused nothing but tension since she got here.

Sean How about that game of cards now that Mammy's up. Edward?

Edward Absolutely. I'm in. John?

Tara What are you asking him for? Sure, you know he doesn't want to join in any of the Christmas festivities.

John I never said that.

Tara You've certainly given that impression. Hasn't he, Mum?

Edie Tara—

Tara She's just too polite to say it. Everyone's just too polite to say it.

Sean Tara!

John To say what?

Tara To say what they're all thinking. That you've ruined Christmas for everybody bringing her here. We've never had any problems before now. We've always spent a perfectly nice, pleasant Christmas together. And suddenly this year, you have to go and ruin it for everybody!

John I'm warning you, Tara—

Edie John! Tara! Stop it! Now!

Rai John, relax.

Tara And you couldn't even have the generosity to pretend to join in because you're afraid of compromising your precious principles in front of your precious woman!

Rai Maybe I'd better leave.

John Don't be silly, Rai. This has nothing to do with you.

Rai No, honestly, I think this was maybe—

Sean Rai, love, please. Sit down. Tara doesn't mean any of that. Do you, Tara?

Tara Yes, I do. If you didn't want to come home for Christmas, you shouldn't have come. No one made you.

John And no one made me bring Rai either?

Tara You said it.

John Ignore her, Rai. She's just bitter because she married a good-for-nothing armchair republican from Belfast and now she's stuck up there with nothing to show for it but a failed marriage and a child who doesn't want to live with her.

Edie John!

Tara Don't you dare talk about Sean Óg like that! You know nothing about my life, John.

John I know enough to know you're jealous of me and Rai. That you're jealous of us having choices, and exercising them. But it isn't my fault you won't move on, Tara. You can't hold me responsible for your lack of courage.

Tara (*close to tears now*) Mum, tell him to shut up!

Edie Daddy's right – why don't we get out the cards and have a nice game of poker.

John What is it about Rai you find so threatening, Tara? Why are you so afraid of her?

Tara Don't you dare patronise me.

Edie Please, John, it's Christmas Day.

Edward Anyone for a chocolate liqueur? Rai?

Rai No, thank you. I think I've upset everybody enough as it is.

Edie Don't be silly, love. You haven't upset anyone. Has she, Sean?

Sean Of course you haven't, love.

Tara (*drunkenly*) Yes, she has! She's upset me! Coming in here with her airs and her graces and her 'I'm not going to mass' and 'I don't like Brussels sprouts!' When she's a bloody visitor in our house, abusing our hospitality!

John How dare you speak about Rai like that!

Rai Maybe she's right, John. Maybe it was a mistake us coming here together. Christmas is a family time, and I'm not family, and … I think maybe I should go.

John Go where?

Rai I don't know – check into a hotel somewhere.

Edie You'll never find a hotel at this time. Not on Christmas night.

John Besides, there's no reason why you should leave just because Tara's drunk. Again.

Tara I am not drunk!

Rai Honestly. I think it'd be for the best.

John Ignore her, Rai.

Rai I still think—

Edward Mum's right, Rai – you'll never get a hotel open around here at this time on Christmas night.

Rai In that case, maybe I'll just go for a bit of a walk. Give you all a chance to spend some time together – just the family. And in the morning I'll call and see about getting an earlier flight back to London.

John Rai, listen. It's just Tara. She's had too much to drink and—

Rai No, John. It's not just Tara. Open your eyes and look at what's staring you in the face. I'll see you later.

John I'll come with you.

Rai No! I just want some time alone, John. (*A beat*) Please. I won't be long.

John *hesitates. A beat.*

Rai Don't wait up for me. I can let myself in.

Rai *smiles awkwardly and exits through the front door. Silence.*

John Well. Merry Christmas to you too, everybody.

Blackout.

Act Three

Scene One

It is the next day – St Stephen's Day. From the radio, a scratchy version of 'Good King Wenceslaus'. **Sean** *sits by the fire doing a crossword.* **John** *paces nervously, edgy. After a couple of seconds, he crosses to the record player and pulls the needle up roughly.* **Sean** *looks up at him, but says nothing. He watches him, concerned, for a couple of seconds, then gets back to his crossword. A pause.* **Edward** *enters stage left.*

Edward Anyone for a turkey and ham sandwich? Da?

Sean I'm grand for the moment.

Edward John?

John No. Thanks.

Sean I'd have another bottle of stout, though. If you're going.

Edward Another bottle of stout. Righto.

Edward *exits in the direction of the kitchen.*

John She must be on that phone now for the best part of an hour. Tara!

Tara (*off*) What?

John How long are you going to be?

Tara (*off*) Not long.

John How long is not long?

Tara (*off*) Oh for Christ's sake – I'll be off in a minute!

John *comes back into the centre of the room.*

Edward Use my mobile.

John It's not about that. What if she's trying to get through?

Sean There's no one she could have stayed with? One of your pals from around here or something?

John She doesn't know anyone in Dublin.

Edward The door wasn't locked by mistake, was it?

John I checked. Christ, if anything's happened to her …

He crosses to the end of the stairs again, increasingly agitated.

John Tara!

Tara (*off*) Two minutes!

Sean Maybe she got on a flight back to London early this morning.

John She'd have called by now. And there's no answer at her flat. Besides, all her stuff's here. Something's happened, I know it has.

Sean Ach, John, sure what can have happened to her around here?

John She's a woman, Da. A black woman. Out on her own on Christmas night. Anything could have happened.

John *crosses to the stairs again.*

John Tara! Get off that fucking phone!

Tara (*appearing*) Jesus, relax – I'm coming!

John About fucking time.

He grabs the cordless phone from **Tara**.

Sean John!

John What?

Sean *makes a 'calm down' motion with his hands.* **John** *shakes his head and crosses to the phone.*

John What number should I ring?

Tara Well it's hardly a 999, is it?

John She's been missing for eighteen hours, Tara.

Tara She's gone off in a huff. Jays, if we went running to the police every time DJ went off in a huff.

Sean (*quickly*) There's a number for the local police station in the front of the book there.

John *takes the book out and finds the number for the local police. He dials the number.*

Tara You don't think you're being a little melodramatic, no?

John No, I don't.

Tara She's a grown woman, John. And a somewhat wilful one at that.

John You don't know anything about her, Tara.

Tara I know she kicked up a big fuss about going to midnight mass when she knew it would mean a lot to—

Sean Tara!

Tara She probably booked into a hotel.

John She'd have rung to let me know.

A beat as **John** *dials. He finishes dialing and looks up at* **Tara**.

John So if the police find her body lying in a ditch somewhere, I hope you'll be pleased with yourself.

Tara *(crossing to pour herself a vodka)* Oh, for God's sake.

There is a ring on the doorbell. **John** *slams the phone down and goes to answer it.*

Tara That's probably her now. With the new boyfriend she picked up on Dun Laoghaire pier.

But it isn't. It's **DJ**, *on a motorised scooter.*

John For fuck's sake, DJ!

DJ What?

John Could you not go round the back, no?

DJ The scooter won't fit past the cars in the garage.

John *shakes his head in irritation as* **DJ** *starts to scoot off stage left.* **John** *goes back to the phone and dials the police again.*

Sean Hold on there a minute – whose scooter is that anyway?

DJ Mine.

Sean Since when?

DJ Since I swapped it with Tommy.

Sean Swapped it? For what?

DJ For a pair of rollerblades.

Sean The rollerblades your mammy and I gave you for Christmas?

DJ Yeah.

And he goes to leave again.

Sean Hold on there now and don't be rushing off anywhere.

(**DJ** *turns wearily to look at* **Sean**) Tommy gave you his scooter for a pair of rollerblades?

DJ Plus fifty euro cash.

Sean Where did you get fifty euro in cash?

DJ Swapped the book token Auntie Kathleen gave me with Graham Finn. And I had thirty euro of my own.

Edward Thirty euro tucked away in a coffee jar under his bed and he buys his presents from the pound shop.

DJ That shaving foam cost me three fifty!

Edward You were robbed, so. You can get it down on Moore Street for a euro.

DJ No, you can't. (*Then, quickly, seeing that* **Sean** *is about to interrogate him further*) Is Rai back yet?

Edward John's on the phone to the police now.

John What the hell's keeping them?

Tara It's Christmas, John. Even the police take time off over Christmas.

DJ Do you want me to go out and have a look for her on my scooter?

John Can't do any harm, I suppose.

Sean Go on, Julian. Get out there and see what you can find.

DJ Right. I'll give yous a bell on the old mobile if I hear anything.

And he scoots off stage left.

Sean I thought he said he couldn't get out through the back door because of the cars in the garage? I'll tell you, that's one little shite—

Sean *is interrupted by another ring on the doorbell.* **John** *slams the phone down and races to open the door. We don't see who it is, but we hear voices off.*

Voices (*singing, off*) The wran the wran,
The King of all birds
St Stephen's Day
Was caught in the furze …

John Fuck off!

And he closes the door in their faces.

Tara John! That was the wran boys!

John *ignores her and takes the phone back off* **Edward**. **Tara** *continues to look at* **John** *for a moment or two, then turns and pours herself another vodka. A beat.*

Sean She'll turn up, John. I promise you. I can feel it in my waters. There'll be some completely innocent explanation.

John I hope you're right. For her sake.

Edward I hope so too. For all our sakes.

And he heads off upstairs.

Tara I don't know why everyone keeps blaming me. All I said was I didn't think Christmas was an appropriate time to bring a stranger into the house. Which it isn't.

Sean You were very hard on her, love. We all were, maybe.

Tara You didn't say anything to her.

Sean No. But I didn't rush in to defend her either.

Tara She doesn't need defending from you, Daddy – she's well able to look after herself, that one.

At that moment, **Edie** *appears dressed in a dressing gown. She looks pale and unwell.*

Sean Hiya, love.

Edie *smiles weakly at him, but says nothing. She crosses to the Christmas tree and plugs the lights out. A beat, as* **Edie** *stands looking up at the top of the tree.*

Edie I wouldn't even have minded if Mammy's Angel had survived.

Sean At least he went quickly, I suppose. Didn't suffer, like.

Edie *throws her husband a look.* **Sean** *looks suitably chastened.* **Edie** *sits wearily in an armchair and stares into the fire.*

Sean Good sleep?

Edie All things considered.

A pause.

Sean Would you like a bit of an oul' turkey sandwich? Edward's done one of his special sauces.

Edie I couldn't stomach anything right now.

Tara Are you all right?

Edie Fine.

Sean *nods. A beat.*

Edie What time of day is it at all?

Sean Just gone two.

Edie Jimmy and Kathleen will be here any minute. (*A beat*) No sign of Rai yet?

Tara Oh for God's sake! Not you as well, Mum!

And with that she disappears up the stairs. A pause.

Sean She's very … angry this weather.

Edie She's missing Sean Óg, that's all.

Sean I hope she's right about Rai.

Edie Sure, what could have happened to her?

Sean Well, you read in the paper about … you know … people being attacked and that. Mugged, or … or … raped. You know – because of …

Edie Because of the colour of their skin?

Sean It happens, you know?

Edie (*shakes head*) That's one cute little madam. She'll have stayed out to teach John a lesson.

Sean You're very hard on her, Edie.

Edie Haven't I a right to be? After she's spoiled our Christmas on us?

Sean Ach now, Edie. It wouldn't be fair to lay all the blame on Rai. We're quite capable of spoiling Christmas on our own.

Edie We always had perfectly peaceful Christmases before she appeared.

Sean Lord God, woman – what planet are you on? I don't think we've ever had a 'perfectly peaceful Christmas' since the day we were married!

Edie We have too!

Sean When? Name one?

Edie We had a lovely Christmas last year.

Sean Edie, we nearly had to call the police on Christmas Eve to separate the two boys when John spilled red wine over Edward's new trousers!

Edie Well, that one incident apart, it was a lovely Christmas.

Sean And you and Julian weren't speaking to one another after he got suspended from school for smoking. And the year before you sulked for the entire Christmas because Edward went skiing in France instead of coming home. And the year before that—

Edie All right! All right! So we've had a few rows! Are you happy now? All families have disagreements – especially at Christmas. That's why I wanted this year to be special! That's why I wanted it to be perfect! That's all I wanted – one perfect Christmas before they're all gone and it's just the two of us again!

She buries her head in her hands, unable to carry on. During the above, **Tara** *has re-entered. She stands watching her parents anxiously. A beat.*

Sean I'm scared for her, Edie, that's all.

Edie It's affected me as well, you know? (*A beat*) But there's nothing we can do except wait and hope and pray that Rai comes back safely.

Sean *crosses to comfort his wife.*

Sean That's the spirit, love. Never say – ah!

Sean *lets out a sudden yelp of pain.*

Tara Dad?

Edie (*rushing over to him, panicky*) Sean? Sean, what's wrong? Have you … ?

Sean (*through gritted teeth*) I think I just stood on a piece of glass!

Edie (*relieved*) Jesus, Sean, you gave me such a fright. I thought you were … here, hold on to me and we'll get you sat down.

Sean *does so, and the two of them hobble awkwardly towards the sofa.* **Tara** *bends and picks up what appears to be a small piece of crystal.*

Tara It's not glass. It's a bit of Mammy's Angel. I must have missed it when I was hoovering up.

Edie *looks up from where she has just deposited* **Sean** *in an armchair.*

Edie Show me? (**Tara** *does so*) That's odd.

Tara What?

Edie Mammy's Angel was made of Waterford Crystal.

Tara So?

Edie Where did you put the remains of the Angel, Tara?

Tara In the bin in the kitchen. Why?

But **Edie***'s gone off stage right, towards the kitchen.*

Tara What's got into her?

Sean Does nobody care about my shredded foot?

Tara Daddy, you're worse than DJ. Sure, it's only an oul' scratch.

Sean An oul' scratch! You wouldn't be calling it an oul' scratch if—

But he gets no further, because **Edie** *is back, carrying several pieces of the broken angel.*

Edie (*cutting across* **Sean**) That wasn't Mammy's Angel on the tree.

Sean What was it, so?

Edie I don't know, but it wasn't Mammy's Angel. Someone's taken Mammy's Angel and replaced it with this … imitation.

Sean Why would anyone want to do that?

Edie I don't know. But they have.

Sean But who … ?

Tara You can't think?

Sean Julian?

Tara Not Julian.

Sean Who then?

Tara Someone we know almost nothing about who came into the house for two days, admired the angel, and then disappeared without trace into the night …

Edie Ah, Tara, don't be ridiculous.

Tara Who's looked down her nose at this family since the moment she walked in, and then took off at the first opportunity?

Edie Tara.

Tara Who coveted everything this family had because she was jealous and her own family were gone off to Kenya for Christmas?

Sean (*incredulous*) Ah, Tara – sure, Rai has better things to be doing than—

At that moment, **John** *appears from upstairs.*

John Than what?

An awkward silence.

John Well?

Sean Nothing, John. It's just Tara being stupid.

Tara How well do you know her, John?

John I beg your pardon?

Edie Tara, please. You're being silly now.

John What's going on?

Sean Don't mind her, John. It's a lot of old nonsense.

Tara This is because she's black, isn't it?

Sean Ach, don't be ridiculous.

Tara It's because she's black no one wants to say what we're all thinking. (*To* **John**) That wasn't the real Mammy's Angel on the top of the tree. Someone switched it for a cheap imitation.

John What's that got to do with … (*He pulls up as it suddenly dawns on him what* **Tara** *is insinuating*) Please tell me you're not suggesting … ?

Edie John, love, no one's suggesting anything.

Tara I'm just asking how well do you know her, John?

John *turns and heads for the stairs.*

The Buddhist of Castleknock

Edie John! John, nobody's saying—

But he's gone. A silence. **Sean** *looks at* **Tara**.

Tara (*defiant*) It's not beyond the realms of possibility, you know. She heard how much it was worth. And *someone's* taken it.

Sean And where would she have got a replacement, tell me that, eh? Sure, they only arrived home the night before last. Do you think she had a spare angel tucked away in her suitcase just in case? It's too ridiculous for words, Tara!

Tara Maybe. But I'm only saying … we know nothing about her. Nothing at all. And who else could have done it?

At that moment, **DJ** *appears.* **Sean** *turns to look at him.*

DJ Still no sign of her.

Sean Julian, look me in the eye and tell me you didn't steal Mammy's Angel.

DJ (*outraged*) I'm not staying to listen to any more of this – I'm out of here!

Edie No you're not. Uncle Jimmy and Auntie Kathleen are due any minute, and you're going to be here to meet them.

DJ No way! I've already arranged to go to Funderland!

Edie Well, you can just un-arrange, because you're not going. You're staying here.

DJ That's not fair! I go every year! It's my Christmas tradition!

Edie Funderland is on all week – you can go some other day.

DJ But all my friends are going today!

Edie I don't care if all your friends are going to the moon and back by dinnertime. You're not. And that's the end of it.

DJ But, Mum—

Edie No buts, Julian. You're staying here to see Uncle Jimmy and Auntie Kathleen and that's it.

DJ For fuck's sake!

Edie Julian!

But **DJ** *has stomped off upstairs.* **Edie** *sighs, agitated.*

Edie I'll murder him one day, I really will.

She breaks off as the phone rings. **Edie** *goes to answer it.*

Edie Hello. (*A beat. Then, frostily*) Ah, Paudge, hello. Happy Christmas to you too. (*A beat*) Ah you know yourself – very quiet. (*A beat*) How's Sean Óg? (*A beat*) Is he? Ah, God love him.

A Beat. **Tara** *enters stage right.*

Edie She is, yes. She's right here beside me, I'll hand her over to you. (*She puts her hand over the phone*) It's Paudge. Is everything all right, love?

The Buddhist of Castleknock

Tara *takes the phone from* **Edie.**

Tara (*terse*) Paudge? Put Sean Óg on. I want to talk to him.

A beat as **Tara** *listens to the response. She motions to her mother that she'll take it upstairs. She exits with the portable phone, crossing* **John** *as he enters pulling on his coat.*

John I'm going out to look for Rai.

Edie Would you not leave that to the police? They have the expertise and the resources and ...

John And what?

Edie Well, not that this is the most important thing – it isn't, but ... well, you know Uncle Jimmy and Auntie Kathleen are on their way over?

John Jesus ...

Edie I couldn't say no, John. They've been coming to our house every St Stephen's Day since we got married. I couldn't call it off at this short notice.

John Mum, Rai has disappeared. She could be lying dead in a gutter somewhere for all we know, and you're going to sit around singing 'Rudolph the Red-Nosed Reindeer' with Jimmy and Kathleen?

Edie Ach, John, love – you're being melodramatic now. If there was any way I could have cancelled it, I would have. I promise you. But I just ...

John Hadn't the courage?

Edie It's not a question of that, John.

John What is it a question of then, Mum?

Edie (*pleading*) A couple of hours, John. That's all I'm asking. You know how much it means to Jimmy and Kathleen. Especially Jimmy – you're his only godson. Please, love …

John Mum …

John *makes for the door as* **Sean** *appears stage left.*

Edie (*desperate*) If Rai's not back by the time Jimmy and Kathleen have gone, we'll all go out looking for her. How about that? (*A beat.* **John** *is wavering*) Please, John. I'm asking you to do this one little thing for me. Please?

At that second, **Tara** *comes running down the stairs in tears.*

Tara The fucking bastard! That fucking, wanking, vindictive little—

Sean *and* **Edward** *come running on to see what the commotion is.*

Tara I'll fucking kill him, I'm telling you! I'll fucking, fucking …

She begins to weep bitterly.

Sean What's wrong, love? What is it?

The Buddhist of Castleknock

Tara Paudge is going off to the Giant's Causeway with his mother and father for the New Year ... and they're taking Sean Óg.

Sean I thought he was supposed to be coming here?

Tara That's not all. Paudge says he's going to fight for custody after all. He says I'm not fit to be a mother.

Edie Why on earth would he say that?

Tara Why do you think, Mum?

Edie Because you like a drink? Sure, we all like a drink.

Tara Yes, but we don't all drink ourslves to sleep with half a bottle of vodka every night.

Sean I never liked that little scut.

Sean takes Tara in his arms.

Sean We'll fight it, love. I promise you. We'll fight it.

There is a ring on the doorbell. A brief pause.

Sean Maybe I should tell Jimmy and Kathleen ...

Tara No! Paudge has done enough damage to our Christmas already.

Sean Are you sure ... ?

Tara I'll let them in.

Tara gets up and goes to answer the door. A beat. **Edie** *looks up at* **John**.

John Look, Mum—

Edie Please, John? A couple of hours?

Before **John** *can reply,* **Jimmy** *and* **Kathleen** *can be heard entering off.*

Jimmy (*singing, off*)   Jingle bells, Santa smells
　　　　　　　　　　　　 Robin flew away
　　　　　　　　　　　　 Kojak lost his lollipop
　　　　　　　　　　　　 And called the IRA – hey!

Tara (*off*) Uncle Jimmy!

Jimmy (*off*) How's my favourite niece?

Tara (*off*) I'm grand altogether. Come on in. How're you, Auntie Kathleen?

Kathleen (*off*) Hello, Tara love.

Enter **Jimmy** *and* **Kathleen** *with* **Tara**. **Jimmy** *is a couple of years older than* **Sean** *– jovial, good-humoured, but not inclined to listen.* **Kathleen** *is* **Edie**'*s older sister – long suffering, but not without humour and intelligence, she is evidently very much used to playing second fiddle to her husband's tomfoolery. Ad-libbed Christmas greetings.*

The Buddhist of Castleknock

Jimmy (*to* **Sean**) Happy Christmas, Sean. Here, have you been singing again?

Sean No, why?

Jimmy You brought the house down!

And he gestures at the hole in the ceiling above the dining room table. He and **Sean** *laugh uproariously.*

Sean The usual?

Jimmy That'd be lovely.

Kathleen (*to* **Edie**) So what happened?

Edie The bath overflowed – you don't want to know. Come on in there and sit down.

Jimmy (*to* **Tara**) Tell us, any word from the young fella?

Tara Yeah, I was talking to him earlier. He's grand. But he's—

Jimmy Did you hear that, Kathleen? I knew that young fella'd be grand. He has his Uncle Jimmy's fighting genes, isn't that right, Tara?

Tara It is indeed, Uncle Jimmy.

Jimmy And how's the man himself? Me favourite godson.

Tara Isn't he your only godson, Uncle Jimmy?

Jimmy He could well be. That doesn't stop him being my favourite, though. You're feeling better, so?

John Sorry?

Jimmy The oul' Arab's belly kept you from midnight mass. Your mother was telling us.

John Was she now?

Jimmy (*winking, conspiratorial*) I blame your father's cheap whiskey. Now if he'd come around to my place for a proper Irish instead of lorrying back that cheap scotch nonsense your father serves …

John Isn't it a pity we didn't.

Jimmy *laughs, delighted.*

Edie (*quickly*) So. How did you get over the Christmas?

Kathleen Ah, you know yourself – very quiet. You?

Edie The same. Very quiet altogether.

Kathleen I must say, Edie, you've the place looking fabulous. Hasn't she, Jimmy?

Jimmy I always say to Kathleen, Edie and Sean always have the most Christmasey house you'll ever see. It makes you feel Christmasey just looking at it.

Edie Well – Tara was a great help.

Kathleen And such a wonderful Christmas tree. Where did you get a tree as solid and as sturdy as that? It looks like it's taken root there in the corner.

Edward That Christmas tree? Sure, that Christmas tree collapsed like a deck of—

Edie (*quickly*) Do you like it? I picked it out myself.

Kathleen Ach, it's gorgeous. We can never get our Christmas tree not to lean. No matter how hard he tries, Jimmy just can't get it to stand up straight.

Jimmy As the actress said about the bishop, wha'? (*To* **John**) Speaking of which where's herself? The oul' girlfriend. Are we not going to meet her, no?

There is an awkward pause.

Jimmy It wasn't a trick question.

John She's—

Edie She's gone out. To visit some relatives of hers in Malahide.

John *stares at* **Edie** *in disbelief. She returns his look, pleading with him silently to say nothing.*

Edie She's due back later. You might meet her.

Jimmy Ah, isn't that a shame? We were dying to meet her, weren't we, Kathleen?

Kathleen We were, of course.

John *makes to exit stage right towards the kitchen.*

Edie Will you have some ice with that, Kathleen? John, get your Auntie Kathleen some ice there like a good man.

John *exits in the direction of the kitchen.* **Jimmy** *waits until he's safely out of earshot before speaking.*

Jimmy So tell us – what's she like? John's fancy woman. Is she a good-looker, she is?

Kathleen Jimmy!

Jimmy I'm only asking. (*To* **Edward**) Eddie – you're a man hasn't lost his appreciation for the fairer sex – what's she like?

Edward Couldn't be nicer. Which is perhaps more than can be said for her hosts.

Jimmy Go on away out of that – she couldn't have come to a more welcoming household, isn't that right, Edie? Tell us, is she blonde? I'd say John's a blonde man now all right.

Edward *turns away from* **Jimmy**. **Jimmy** *barely notices.*

Edie So tell us, Jimmy—

Tara She's black. Of African extraction, I think the correct phrase is these days.

Edie Tara!

Tara I'm not saying there's anything wrong with that. But you can't deny the fact.

Edie I just don't see that it's relevant.

Jimmy You're having me on?

Tara Scout's honour. (*She glances towards the door to make sure* **John** *is still out of earshot, then turns back to* **Jimmy**) And the reason he didn't go to midnight mass is because he's become a Buddhist.

Jimmy No!

Tara Cross my heart and hope to die.

A beat. **Jimmy** *looks around incredulously for confirmation of this revelation.* **Sean** *looks away as* **Edie** *smiles awkwardly.*

Jimmy A bloody Buddhist, wha'? Isn't that a good one!

Kathleen Now, Jimmy—

Sean Well, each to his own, as the fella says.

At that moment, **John** *arrives back with the ice.*

Jimmy There he is – the man himself. The Buddhist of Castleknock, wha'?

Jimmy *laughs raucously at his own wit.* **John** *glares at* **Edie**.

Jimmy Come on in here, Johnny boy, and give us a go on your magic carpet!

And he starts to guffaw again. The others eye **John** *warily, wondering how he will react to* **Jimmy***'s teasing.* **Edie**, *in particular, catches his eye with an imploring look that says 'Please just grin and bear it – for me'. A silence. At length* **Jimmy** *stops laughing.*

Jimmy Ah, here. I'm only joking you, Johnny boy. Sure, each to his own, as your daddy says. Isn't that right, Kathleen?

Kathleen It is. And you'd do well to remember that.

Jimmy Sure, I was only joking. John knows that, don't you, John?

John *just smiles. A pause.*

Edie Edward, fix your Uncle Jimmy another whiskey there like a good lad, will you?

Edward *crosses to the drinks cabinet and starts to pour a whiskey for* **Jimmy**.

Jimmy Good man yourself, Eddie.

There is a slightly awkward pause as **John** *and* **Edward** *fix the drinks and hand them out.*

Tara Speaking of joking, tell us the one about the Pope dying again there, Uncle Jimmy.

Edie Oh yes, I love that story – how does it go again?

Jimmy Ach, ye don't want to be hearing that old story again, do ye?

The Buddhist of Castleknock

Tara 'Course we do, Jimmy. Don't we, Da?

Sean I'm not sure we have much choice, do we?

Tara How does it start again, Jimmy?

Jimmy Well, it starts with the two fellas working at the Vatican – the Irish fella and the English fella, and – ah here, sure I've told ye this story hundreds of times. Doesn't anyone have a Christmas joke?

Tara We can tell Christmas jokes afterwards. After the Vatican story.

Jimmy (*sighs*) Well, the Irish fella and the English fella are working away in the kitchens of the Vatican when word comes through that the Pope is after dyin'. And all the staff are sent home until they can pick a new Pope. Because it's an awful complicated process picking a new Pope, so they have to close the whole of the Vatican down until they can pick one. Is that the right word? 'Pick'? What's the word I'm looking for?

Edward Elect.

Jimmy Good man yourself, Eddie – that's the word. They have to close the Vatican down while they elect a new Pope. Jays, how did I forget that word?

Kathleen God, Jimmy – would you ever get on with it. We'll be here all night.

Jimmy Right so, where was I? Oh yes, the two lads are after being sent home while they elect a new Pope in the Vatican.

Only before they go, they're warned not to breathe a word to anyone. They want to have the replacement Pope all lined up, d'you see, before they announce that the old Pope is dead – for the purposes of continuity, and the well-being of the flock and all that kind of thing, d'you know?

Tara I love this story.

Jimmy So now home they go, the Irish fella and the English fella, and on the plane home, the Irish fella, being a betting man, he says to the English fella, 'I'll tell you now, William what we'll do,' says he. 'You go back to London, and I'll go back to Galway, and we'll raise every penny we can lay our hands on and put a bet on the Pope being dead within the next month, and think of the odds we'll get! We'll make a fortune.' And the English fella thinks this is a great idea altogether, and this is what they'll do. And so off they go their separate ways. Anyways, the two lads lose touch, and ten years later, the English fella finds himself in Galway on business – 'cos he's a multi-millionaire now, like, after mortgaging his house, and his mother's house, and his sister's house, and everyone belonging to him's house, and putting the whole lot on the Pope being dead within the month at odds of a thousand to one. But when he eventually finds his old mate Mick from the Vatican and pays him a visit in his top-of-the-range Rolls Royce, isn't Mick living in a tiny hovel, without a penny to his name except what he makes begging in Galway town. And the English fella is amazed, and he says to Mick (*affects English accent*) 'What happened, Mick,' he says – (*normal accent*) he was English, you know? 'What happened Mick,' he says. 'Did you not do the same as me and put every penny you could lay your hands on on the Pope being dead within a month and become a multi-millionaire overnight like I did myself?' And

The Buddhist of Castleknock

Mick looks at him sadly and says he, 'I did,' he says. 'I raised every penny I could lay me hands on. But do you know,' he says, 'when it came to putting the bet on, I couldn't resist a double with the Archbishop of Canterbury!'

Tara *and* **Edie** *laugh delightedly at the punchline.* **Kathleen** *smiles, obviously proud of her husband's ability to tell a joke and hold an audience. Even* **Edward** *and* **Sean** *can't help smiling. Only* **John***'s smile seems forced, unnatural.*

Jimmy You'll never get the Irish out of Ireland, hah!

Tara The Archbishop of Canterbury! I love that story!

Edward (*dry*) It must be the way he tells them.

Edie God, I love a good laugh at Christmas. Does anyone know any Christmas jokes? Edward, you must have an old Christmas joke for us.

Edward I didn't think they came much older than Uncle Jimmy's joke.

Edie How about you, Tara? Do you know any Christmas jokes, love?

Tara Ach, I'm no good at telling jokes, Mum. Sure, you know that.

John I'll tell you a Christmas joke.

Jimmy Good man yourself, John. (*Winks at* **Tara**) Who said Buddhists have no sense of humour, wha'?

Edie (*quickly*) Go on, John. Give us your Christmas joke.

Jimmy Ciúnas. Ciúnas. Whist now for the Buddhist of Castleknock!

Kathleen Jimmy! Be quiet!

John Well there was this family – 'd'you see' – a normal, run-of-the-mill, middle-class family—

Jimmy Like ourselves!

Kathleen Whist now, Jimmy – you've had your chance. Go on, John.

John Well, there was this ordinary middle-class family – from Castleknock, say – and whenever anyone would ask them the question, 'How did you get over the Christmas', they would always reply with the same stock answer: 'Ah, you know yourself – very quiet'.

Jimmy 'Tis true for you. That's what people always say, all right. 'Ah, very quiet.'

Kathleen Jimmy!

John And begob, it didn't matter if the Christmas was, for the sake of argument, very loud; or very raucous; or full of intrigue and surprise and extraordinary occurences which wouldn't look out of place in a murder mystery novel; whenever anyone asked any member of this Castleknock family 'How did you get over the Christmas' – an interesting turn of phrase in itself, incidentally, likening the Yuletide period, as it does, to a particularly virulent bout of yellow fever – but whenever any member of this model family was asked 'How did you get over the Christmas', each and every one of them could be relied upon to trot out the old refrain – Edward?

Edward Ah, you know yourself – very quiet.

John Got it in one. In fact, I think one could safely say that were a murder to be committed in this family on Christmas Day itself—

Edward Not an improbable event, in all fairness.

John Or a rape, say, or any other … atrocity – one suspects that the answer to the question 'How did you get over the Christmas?' would remain mercifully unaltered.

Jimmy (*delighted*) It would too! He's dead right!

John So despite the fact that it was a good ten to fifteen years since this model family from Castleknock had got as far as the second course of their annual Christmas dinner without someone leaving the table in tears, or someone punching someone else—

Edie Please, John—

John Or, as happened on one memorable occasion, the police nearly being called when one member of the family spilled red wine on the new trousers of another member of the family – sorry about that, by the way, Edward—

Edward Please, don't mention it.

John Thereby adding to the kerfuffle before dinner even began when yet another member of the family – who probably should have known better – rather overdid the Christmas cheer and had to have her stomach pumped—

Tara You bastard.

John Still, even on this most unquiet year, the family from Castleknock trotted off to midnight mass together and stood around cheerfully afterwards in the canary yellow earmuffs the youngest member of the family had bought them each as a special Yuletide gift the year before, telling any friends and neighbours who would care to listen that Christmas had indeed been very quiet.

Edward (*tugging his forelock*) You know yourself.

DJ *appears down the stairs to see what's going on.*

John Ah, DJ. The donator of the yellow earmuffs himself. You're just in time to hear the end of my joke.

Jimmy *Is* there an end to this joke? Because I, for one, am getting—

John Oh yes, we're building nicely to the climax now. Because one year, it came to pass that a new element was added to the mix, which was to spoil the carefully balanced cake completely. Think, if you will, of what might happen if you added gelagnite instead of gelatine—

Edward Semtex instead of sugar?

John Armalites in place of armagnac?

The Buddhist of Castleknock

Edward   Machetes in place of marzipan?

DJ   What are they talking about?

John   Excellent, DJ. A fine and worthy contribution to the conversation. What indeed?

Sean   John—

John   Well, the point is that no longer could this family from Castleknock – let's call them the Castles—

Edward   The Castles from Castleknock? I like it.

John   No longer could the Castles convince themselves—

Edward   Or by extension others—

John   That their Christmas – or indeed their lives – were very quiet. Because although this new presence wasn't like them – begob, the poor deluded thing didn't even celebrate Christmas –

Edward   Shame!

John   But worse – she had turned the head of one of the family's favoured sons and brainwashed him into an almost cavalier casting off of God and country—

Edward   God bless Ireland!

John   Of nationhood and religion, of tradition and customs which so enraged the Castles from Castleknock that they turned on the devil incarnate, and froze her out, and took every opportunity to point out that she was, as she knew herself to be deep down, an outsider, an interloper, a queer and dangerous influence—

Edie John, please – stop it!

John Until finally she could take no more, and the poor woman – herself brought up on fables and stories of a sceptred isle of a hundred thousand welcomes and blessings – the poor woman fled, and the Castles were sad, and mourned dutifully, but not enough to halt the refrain 'Ah, you know yourself, very quiet' or to stop them inviting their favourite uncle who nobody liked because he was a small-minded, racist bigot—

Edward Easy, John …

A beat. **John** *looks at* **Edward**, *then across at* **Jimmy** *with barely disguised contempt.* **Edie** *is in tears now, her head in her hands.*

Jimmy Go on, John.

John That's it. That's the end of the joke.

A pause.

DJ I don't get it. (*A beat*) Where's the punchline?

John You're the punchline, DJ. And thank Christ we've got you, or we'd all have gone mad years ago.

A silence. At length, **Kathleen** *speaks.*

Kathleen I think … I think we should go.

Tara But we haven't had our sing-song!

Kathleen I don't think anyone's really in the mood for a sing-song right now, Tara, love.

Tara Why, because John's turned into a miserable, bitter little misanthrope? You're not going to let that spoil our Christmas sing-song, are you? Uncle Jimmy?

Jimmy (*looking straight at* **John**) I'll give yous a song.

Kathleen Jimmy, please—

Jimmy Tara's right. It'd be shame to allow our good-natured annual sing-song to be … sabotaged. Johnny boy? You wouldn't object to one song now, would you?

John *shrugs.*

Edie Jimmy please, don't—

Jimmy Good man yourself. We can salvage something from our Stephen's Day yet.

Tara Go on, so, Jimmy – give us your song. And I'll fix us all another drink.

Jimmy It's more of a poem, now, though, than a song.

Tara A poem. Sure, we love poetry in this house, don't we, Eddie?

Edward Love it? We live it, Tara. Our lives are just one long Gaelic lament.

Jimmy Fair enough, so.

Jimmy *clears his throat and starts to recite the Luke Kelly poem, 'For What Died the Sons of Róisín'. He begins in an almost gay, jovial manner, a grotesque parody of the gravelly-throated Dublin poet. But as the poem progresses, he becomes more focused, less showy, more intent. He keeps a close eye on* **John** *throughout the recitation. But* **John***'s face betrays no emotion. Instead, he continues to look down at the floor throughout.*

Jimmy   For what died the sons of Róisín, was it fame?
For what died the sons of Róisín, was it fame?
For what flowed Ireland's blood in rivers,
That began when Brian chased the Dane,
And did not cease nor has not ceased,
With the brave sons of '16,
For what died the sons of Róisín, was it fame?

For what died the sons of Róisín, was it greed?
For what died the sons of Róisín, was it greed?
Was it greed that drove Wolfe Tone
to a pauper's death in a cell of cold wet stone?
Will German, French or Dutch inscribe
the epitaph of Emmet?
When we have sold enough of Ireland
to be but strangers in it.
For what died the sons of Róisín, was it greed?

To whom do we owe our allegiance today?
To whom do we owe our allegiance today?
To those brave men who fought and died
that Róisín live again with pride?
Her sons at home to work and sing,
Her youth to dance and make her valleys ring,

Or the faceless men who for mark and dollar,
Betray her to the highest bidder,
To whom do we owe our allegiance today?

For what suffer our patriots today?
For what suffer our patriots today?
They have a language problem, so they say,
How to write 'No Trespass'
must grieve their heart full sore,
We got rid of one strange language
now we are faced with many, many more,
For what suffer our patriots today?

Sin a bhfuil.

There is a tense pause at the end of **Jimmy***'s recital. Nobody is quite sure how to react.*

John (*quiet*)   I'm going out to look for Rai.

He crosses to get his coat. The others watch him go.

Edie   Wait!

They all turn to look at her in surprise.

Edie   I'm sorry, Kathleen, but I think you and Jimmy should leave.

Jimmy   Edie?

Edie   We'd like to be left alone now. As a family.

Jimmy Edie, I didn't start it.

Edie I'd like you to leave all the same.

Jimmy *looks at her, then nods slowly.*

Jimmy Fair enough. (*He crosses to get his coat, brushing past* **John** *as he does so*) Are you right, Kathleen?

And he disappears out the front door. A pause, as **Kathleen** *puts on her coat.*

Edie I'm sorry, Kathleen.

Kathleen I understand, love.

Edie I'll call over in the next day or two.

Kathleen Do that. (*A beat*) And thanks for your hospitality.

Jimmy (*off*) Kathleen.

Kathleen I'll see you all soon.

And she follows **Jimmy** *off. A silence.*

John I'm sorry, everybody. For ruining your afternoon.

Edie You didn't ruin anything, John. It was Jimmy ruined it.

John Still and all ... I'm sorry.

A pause.

Edie We're sorry too, love.

Tara Are we?

Edie For not being more accommodating. Aren't we, Sean?

Sean We are. And for putting you through that.

John Ach ...

Another long pause.

John You know, you're not meant to get attached to things as a Buddhist. (*A beat*) Looks like I'm going to make an even worse Buddhist than I did a Catholic.

Edie We'll find her, John. I promise you we'll find her. Come on, everybody. Get your coats.

Tara Where are we going?

Edie We're going out to look for Rai. All of us. Come on. Get your coats and let's go.

Tara *is about to protest, but something in* **Edie**'*s voice, and the events of the past couple of minutes, make her think better of it. She hesitates a beat, then crosses and exits.* **Sean** *follows her, as does* **Edward**. **DJ** *heads towards the kitchen.*

Edie Where do you think you're going?

DJ I'm going to tell Tommy I can't go to Funderland! God!

Edie As long as you're not trying to get out of looking for Rai.

DJ I don't want to get out of looking for Rai. I was the one out looking for her while yous were all sitting around talking shite with Uncle Jimmy!

Edie It's true for you. Go on, tell Tommy you can't go to Funderland and let's get cracking.

DJ *and* **Edie** *exit, leaving* **John** *alone on the stage. He sits by the fire, exhausted and dejected, his head in his hands. After a couple of seconds* **Edward** *appears, holding his coat. He stands for a moment watching his brother, wanting desperately to reach out to him, but unsure of how to go about it. Eventually,* **John** *looks up and sees him. He smiles a forced, tired smile at his brother. A pause.*

Edward That snow is coming down heavy now. Looks like it's going to stick. If only it had come yesterday. Mum would have had her dream white Christmas.

John If it had come yesterday, Rai could well have frozen to death by now.

Edward I'm sorry, I didn't …

John 'S all right. (*A beat*) Jesus, Edward – if anything's happened to her …

And he starts to cry silently. **Edward** *crosses and puts his arm around* **John**, *who buries his head in his brother's chest.* **DJ** *appears back into the living room carrying his jacket.*

DJ God, look at yis! Not only is me sister turning into me mother, but I've a pair of fuckin' queers for brothers! No wonder I failed my Junior Cert!

Edie (*appearing back*) Julian!

DJ I don't believe it – she's everywhere!

Edward Omnipresent is the word you're looking for Jules. Like the Buddah.

DJ Not you as well! Jaysus!

Edie Right. Come on, the lot of you, and let's get a move on.

The family starts to make its way towards the front door. But just as **Edie** *is opening the door, the phone rings.* **Sean** *is closest to it and he picks it up. The others watch him intently.*

Sean Just one moment. (*Holds phone out to* **John**) It's the police.

John *glances nervously at his mother, before crossing to take the receiver from* **Edward**.

John Hello? Yes, that's right. (*A beat*) Is she all right? (*A beat*) I'll come straight up. Thank you. (*He puts the phone down and looks up at the others, numb*) They've found Rai. They've taken her up to the hospital.

Edie Jesus, Mary and Joseph. Is she …?

John They don't know. She's still unconscious.

Edward Come on – I'll run you up to the hospital.

Edward *grabs his coat and follows* **John** *out the front door. A silence.* **Edie** *sinks into the nearest armchair.* **Tara** *crosses to sit on the arm of the chair.* **Sean** *and* **DJ** *stand in silent shock as the lights fade slowly to black.*

Blackout.

Act Three

Scene Two

In the blackout, a loud and bracing rendition of 'We Wish You a Merry Christmas'. When the lights eventually come up, it is a week or so later. **Edward** *stands looking out of the window as* **Sean** *reads his paper.* **Tara** *appears stage left. She is clearly tense, agitated.*

Tara Has anybody seen Rai's jacket?

Sean Did John not take it up to the hospital to her?

Tara Would I be looking for it if he had?

A beat.

Sean I wonder what's keeping them?

Tara John rang to say they'd be delayed. The police were still taking statements and that.

Sean They'll miss their flights if they're not careful.

Tara That's why I'm packing Rai's bags for her. Give them a head start.

Sean Poor Rai. Wasn't much of a holiday for her, was it? Beaten to a pulp by a crowd of gurriers, followed by three days above in the hospital.

Tara On her first visit here too. No doubt now she'll leave thinking we're all like those … animals.

Edward No doubt.

Tara How was she when you went up?

Sean I never got in to see her. The nurse said she wasn't really up to having visitors, only John. And sure, could you blame her after what happened?

Tara Well – it's up to us to redress the balance by showing her some honest to goodness Irish hospitality for the few minutes they'll have left. Is the kettle on?

And she exits towards the kitchen, left. A beat.

Edward She's changed her tune.

A pause. **Sean** *sighs deeply and looks at his watch. Suddenly, he looks like an old man.*

Sean I'm telling you, if I ever lay my hands on the bastards attacked her, they'll not get away from me alive. So help me God.

Edward Well, let he who is without sin …

Sean This is it. (*A beat.* **Sean** *looks at his watch*) They won't even have time for a cup of tea in the hand if they don't hurry up. (*Another beat*) I think I'll maybe go and help Tara with the tea. Give myself something to do, d'you know?

Sean *exits towards the kitchen.* **Edward** *lies heavily on the couch and closes his eyes. After a couple of seconds,* **DJ** *appears in from the hallway. He looks around furtively, decides that the room is empty, then hurries over to the Christmas tree. He pulls up a chair, takes another look around to satisfy himself that no one is coming, then pulls Mammy's Angel from under his jumper. He quickly puts the Angel on the top of the tree, then disappears out of the room post-haste. After a couple of seconds,* **Edward** *speaks.*

Edward Careful you don't drop that, DJ. It must be worth – ooh, the price of a motorised scooter I'd say?

DJ *stops.*

DJ I swapped it back. Satisfied?

Edward If you'd only waited till the Christmas decorations had been taken down, no one would have been any the wiser till this time next year.

DJ Jaysus, no wonder I'm a juvenile delinquent with an older brother like you!

And he heads off stage left, passing **Sean** *as he goes.*

Sean Where are you … ?

But **DJ** *is gone.* **Sean** *might follow him, but he is distracted by the sound of* **Edie**, **John** *and* **Rai** *returning.*

Edie (*off*) Mind yourself there now.

Sean *turns to put the biscuits he is carrying down on the sideboard.*

Sean (*to* **Edward**)　Return of the war heroine, wha'?

He pulls up as **Rai** *comes into the living room, helped by* **Edie** *and* **John**. **Rai** *walks using a single crutch. Her face and neck are heavily bandaged, and her face is swollen and bruised. Her free arm is in a sling. Her voice, when she speaks, is cracked and weak.*

Sean　Good Jesus ...

Rai　Not even a pretty face any more.

At that moment **Tara** *bursts in. She too pulls up as she sees the extent of the damage.*

Rai　It's not as bad as it looks. The crutch is only temporary.

Sean *shakes his head in disbelief. Another silence.*

Sean　What did the Guards say?

John　They didn't hold out much hope of catching them.

Sean　How many of them were there?

Rai　Three or four – it's hard to tell when you're curled up in a ball trying to protect yourself from being kicked to death.

Sean　All young fellas?

Rai *nods.*

Edie　It'd frighten you, wouldn't it? For the future of the country. When the young people are ...

She trails off, unable to bring herself to continue.

Edward (*gentle*)　It isn't off the ground they licked it, Mum …

Edie　No. No, I suppose it isn't.

Sean (*to* **Rai**)　Some memories you'll take home of the land of Saints and Scholars. You'll be glad to see the back of it.

Rai　It'll pass. One day. One day I might even want to come back. (*To* **John**) Did you book the taxi?

Tara　Edward's offered to give us a lift.

Rai　Damn police kept haranguing me for every last detail. Where was I going when it happened, what was I doing in the park. Had I provoked them. I told them I didn't see them, and I've no idea where I was going – I've never even been to this damn country before in my life. But they didn't seem to get it. Or if they got it, they weren't that interested.

Sean　What did they say? Did they think they'd catch them?

Rai　They said they'd investigate. But I ain't holding my breath.

John　The Guards said they're dealing with this kind of thing three or four times a week.

Edward (*facetious*)　Even in Castleknock?

A pause.

Rai I'd better get a move on or we'll miss the flight.

John I'll give you a hand.

Rai Thank you.

John *crosses and puts his arm around* **Rai***'s shoulder, and they make as if to exit to the hall.*

Tara (*awkward*) Actually, I … took the liberty of packing your bags for you. I hope you don't mind. I just thought with you being in a hurry, and just arriving back from the hospital and … Well – I hope you don't mind.

A beat as **Rai** *looks at her.*

Rai Thanks, Tara. Thank you.

A pause.

Edward Well, if you'll excuse me. In the absence of someone to pack my bags for me, I'd better get a move on.

Edward *disappears into the hall and up the stairs.*

John I'll get our stuff.

He gently manouevres **Rai** *into an armchair by the fire, then turns and exits into the hall.*

Edie Sean, run up there and help John. I'll make us a quick cup of tea in the hand.

And she exits left as **Sean** *disappears up the stairs, leaving* **Rai** *and* **Tara** *alone together. An awkward silence.*

Tara I meant what I said earlier. I really am sorry.

A beat. **Rai** *acknowledges the apology in silence.*

Rai (*eventually*) I heard about ... your ex-husband ... wanting to keep your baby and that.

Tara Yes.

Rai I'm very sorry.

Tara Thank you.

Rai If there's anything we can do, me and John ... you know?

Tara I'm going up there now. His parents have a mobile home near the Giant's Causeway. If he thinks he's going to take Sean Óg off me without a fight, he's got another thing coming.

Rai Attah girl. You fight your corner. (*A beat*) Good luck, yeah?

Tara Thank you.

Another pause.

Rai Did you know there's a Tara in Tibetan Buddhist mythology? Two, actually. White Tara and Green Tara.

Tara I always thought Tara was an Irish name.

Rai Maybe. But according to the Mahayana scriptures, the Enlightened Being Chenrezi was given the task of rescuing all living beings from *samsara* – the cycle of endless rebirth – and helping them to reach nirvana. But the task was so onerous he became exhausted and depressed, and cried great tears of despair which fell to the ground and grew into lotus flowers. From these lotus flowers were born the enlightened beings Green Tara and White Tara, whose destiny was to assist Chenrezi in his work and become symbols of the Buddha's great compassion towards all people.

Tara The patron saint of compassion, hah? Who'd have thought it?

Rai Sean Óg, for one.

Tara Maybe.

Rai I've heard the way you talk about him. He's a very lucky boy.

Tara Thank you.

At that moment **Edie** *appears with a mug of tea.*

Edie There you go, Rai. Excuse the presentation.

Rai *takes the tea from* **Edie**. **John** *appears in from the hall carrying two large bags.*

John I think that's the lot.

Tara (*to* **Rai**) You don't mind me coming as far as the train station with you?

Rai Of course not.

Rai *smiles at* **Tara**, *who smiles back awkwardly. Nobody is quite sure what to say next.*

Rai Before we go – I got you a little thank you present. For having me. It's nothing big – just a little something for the household.

Edie Ah, Rai – did you hear that, Sean? Rai got us a present.

Rai (*rummaging in the front compartment of her bag*) I wanted to give it to you before I left.

Edie Rai, love, that's very kind of you. (*Reading the tag on the present*) 'A little something no Christian home should be without. Happy New Year. Love, Rai'.

Rai If you don't like it John and I can bring it back.

Edie *pulls open the packaging. An ornamental statue of the Bodhisattva Kuan-Yin falls out into her lap.*

Edie It's absolutely gorgeous. Isn't it gorgeous, Sean?

Sean It certainly is.

Edie Oh Rai, it really is beautiful. (*A beat*) What is it?

Sean Ach, Edie, can you not see what it is? It's a Buddha.

Rai It's a Bodhisattva, actually. That's like the next one down from a Buddha.

John A Bodhisattva is a kind of Buddha who has stayed behind to help the rest of us lesser mortals to reach Nirvana.

Rai This one is a Chinese Boddhisatva called Kuan Yin. (*To Tara*) The Chinese version of Chenrezi. (*To the others*) It means literally, 'taking heed of the sound'. Chinese Buddhists believe she watches over the world listening to its cries and saving people from pain and anguish and disease.

Sean A sort of a Buddhist Mary, wha'?

Rai If you like.

Edie It's beautiful, Rai. And a lovely gesture.

Edward And one, I might suggest, of which we are entirely undeserving.

Rai Well – it's just something I ... wanted you to have ...

A pause.

Edward Right. I hate to break up the party, but it's time we were making a move.

Sean All good things, hah? No getting away from it.

Tara No. See you, Mum.

And she gives **Edie** *a kiss.*

Edie Goodbye, Tara, love.

Tara Shit. I think I'm going to cry.

Edie Go on – don't be getting me started.

Tara Bye, Dad.

Sean Bye, love. And good luck with Paudge.

Edward Are you right? See you, Mum.

Edie (*to* **Edward**, *giving him a hug*) Goodbye, love.

And **Edward** *heads for the front door.*

Tara Thanks for a … lovely Christmas, Mum.

Edward You're going to miss your train, Tara.

Tara Right.

And she turns and follows **Edward** *out into the hall.* **Edie** *sees them out.*

John Take care of yourself, Dad.

Sean You too. And take care of Rai.

John I will.

John *holds out his hand for a handshake. A beat, before* **John** *leans forward and gives* **Sean** *a very tentative, very awkward hug. By now* **Edie** *has returned.* **John** *turns to her.*

John Bye, Mum.

Edie Goodbye, love.

John *hugs her. They hold one another for some time. Meanwhile,* **Sean** *comes up to* **Rai**.

Sean Will you come and see us again sometime?

Rai Who knows? If I'm invited.

Sean You're welcome here anytime, Rai. Isn't she, Edie?

Edie Of course you are, Rai, love.

Rai Goodbye, Mrs Sullivan. And thank you.

Edie No, Rai. Thank you.

A beat. **Rai** *turns and starts to hobble towards the door, helped by* **John**.

Rai Say goodbye to DJ for us.

Sean If we can find him.

Sean *and* **Edie** *stand as we hear the noise of the others getting into the car, etc., off. Ad libbed goodbyes from* **Edie** *and* **Sean** *as we hear the car pulling off.*

Edie Well. That's it. Just the three of us again.

Sean Thanks be, as the fella says, to the Divine Jaysus.

Edie (*with less conviction than usual*) Sean!

Sean Well, they're more trouble than they're worth. I mean, what's the reward for twenty years of hard labour? The prospect of a whole load more of them in their own images getting under your feet every Christmas? Good riddance, I say.

A beat.

Edie (*picking up the Bodhisattva*)   Kuan Yin. She who takes heed of the sound.

Sean   You've a great memory for names all the same, Edie.

Edie   Sure, didn't I spend my youth remembering the names of the saints? One little Chinese saint isn't going to baffle me at this stage of my life. What about putting her here on the mantlepiece? Or how about …

Edie *looks about the room for a suitable resting place for Kuan Yin. She stops short as she notices that the angel her mother gave her is back on the top of the tree.*

Sean   What?

Edie   Mammy's Angel. He's back on the top of the tree. How did he … ?

Edie *and* **Sean** (*together*)   Julian!

Sean   The little shite!

A beat.

Sean   Better late than never, I suppose.

A pause.

Edie (*eventually*) You know, Sean, maybe Mammy's Angel has had her day.

Sean How do you mean?

Edie Well, maybe its time we gave someone else a go at the top of the tree.

Sean Kuan Yin?

Edie There's no harm in seeing what it looks like …

Sean There is not. No harm at all.

Edie And she *is* sitting, so it might look very …

Sean Appropriate?

Edie You never know. Besides, there's no law says she has to stay there if we don't like it.

Edie *hands him the nearest chair.* **Sean** *positions the chair and carefully takes the angel from the top of the tree, replacing it with the statue of Kuan Yin. He gets back down and the two of them stand for a second or two looking up at the top of the tree.*

Edie What do you think?

Sean Not bad. It's not your mother's angel, but … mm – not bad at all.

Edie I think she looks as if she was born like that.

The Buddhist of Castleknock

Sean What, with the tip of a Christmas tree up her arse?

Edie Sean! No ... sitting cross-legged and serene on top of her perch, surveying the world and listening to its cries.

Sean (*teasing*) You're not thinking of converting ... ?

Edie I'm too old to be thinking of converting to new religions, Sean. I'm only just over what the nuns did to me.

Edie *sits back on the sofa. A pause as they sit looking up at the statue of Kuan Yin on the top of the tree. The lights start to fade very slowly – almost imperceptibly – from now until the end of the play, accentuating the glow of the fairy lights on the Christmas tree, and* **Rai**'s *Boddhisatva perched on the top.*

Edie It wasn't a complete disaster, was it, Sean?

Sean No. Not a complete disaster.

Edie I just so desperately wanted it to be nice for them. That's all I cared about. I wanted it to be nice for them. And for you. In case it's our last Christmas ...

Sean Edie, it was a lovely Christmas. And please God, we'll have many more just like it. (*A beat*) Well ... maybe not just like it.

Edie *laughs gently. A beat.*

Sean It might be hard to believe right at this moment, but who knows – in years to come, maybe we'll look back on this as our best Christmas ever.

Edie *smiles wearily at him.*

Edie Maybe.

They hold one another's gaze for a couple of seconds, then start to kiss, a long passionate kiss one suspects they haven't experienced in some time. After a few seconds, **DJ** *appears in from the hall, unnoticed by either* **Edie** *or* **Sean**.

DJ Oh my God! Youse two are dis-gusting!

Blackout.